IT IS DOUBTFUL whether, in British parliamentary history, there has ever been a more fascinating struggle between two rival political leaders than the great duel which took place between Gladstone and Disraeli in the latter half of the nineteenth century.

Rarely have two great statesmen, living at the same time, been so dissimilar. Gladstone, a Scot, was educated at Eton and Oxford; he had no difficulty in obtaining a seat in the Commons, as a Tory, when barely twenty-three. Disraeli, a Jew, left school at fifteen; he tried four times to enter Parliament before being successful and was laughed down during his maiden speech. Surprisingly it was Disraeli who became leader of the 'aristocratic' party, while Gladstone headed the Liberals.

This book, though briefly tracing the early careers of these men, is mainly concerned with the period from 1852 to 1881. What were the major issues which confronted the men at Westminster during these years? Why did they generate so much political heat both within Parliament and outside? Contemporary sources have been used to supply answers to these questions; included are edited extracts from parliamentary debates, government reports, speeches, diaries, letters, newspapers, novels, poems, songs, pamphlets, etc.

Illustrated throughout with pictures drawn from contemporary sources, this addition to the WAYLAND DOCUMENTARY HISTORY SERIES, offers an exciting and authentic approach to history studies.

Frontispiece The 'Choice of Hercules', or an impossible choice for
England between the policies of Gladstone and Disraeli

PEACE & PROSPERITY

PEACE & EMPIRE

SWAIN SC

Gladstone and Disraeli

'Lord Beaconsfield [Disraeli] and Mr Gladstone are incomparably the two most distinguished public men of our epoch. Their national services are great; their political calibre is unapproached by any one of their contemporaries.' *The Standard* 30 March 1881.

by Patrick Rooke

WAYLAND PUBLISHERS LONDON

Second impression 1973

Copyright © 1970 by Wayland (Publishers) Ltd.
101 Grays Inn Road, London, WC1

SBN (hardback edition): 85340 010 5
SBN (paperback edition): 85340 283 3

Filmset and printed in Great Britain by
BAS Printers Limited, Wallop, Hampshire

Contents

The Illustrations

1 Early Days

AT THE BEGINNING of the nineteenth century, Britain was on the threshold of great change. The economic effects of the French wars, which had led to the introduction of income tax, were accompanied by the impact of the Industrial and Agricultural Revolutions. The population was on the move and new towns were growing rapidly. At the same time, a deep current of social unrest was running through the land. Poverty was a major problem. Through strikes and riots workers were showing more and more dissatisfaction with the conditions under which they laboured, and even many of the prosperous middle classes were resentful that they were not allowed to vote at parliamentary elections. It was into such a social scene that Benjamin Disraeli and William Gladstone were born.

Never in British parliamentary history has there been a more fascinating struggle between two political leaders than the great duel which took place between Gladstone and Disraeli in the latter half of the nineteenth century. Rarely have two British statesmen, confronting each other on the floor of the House of Commons, been so dissimilar. Gladstone, a Scot, was educated at Eton and Oxford; he had no difficulty in obtaining a seat in Parliament, as a Tory, when barely twenty-three. Disraeli, a Jew, left school at fifteen; he tried four times to enter the House before being successful and was laughed down during his maiden speech. Yet, oddly enough, it was Disraeli who became leader of the 'aristocratic' party, while Gladstone headed the Liberals.

Each was an outstanding politician who commanded the respect and loyalty of a big following, both inside and outside

The great duel

11

Facing page The New Houses of Parliament, built during the reign of Queen Victoria

Parliament. Their rivalry caught the imagination of the public and awakened an interest in political affairs which has seldom been matched since.

Mutual dislike
In a letter to Queen Victoria, dated 24 April 1880, Lord Grenville wrote: 'Lord Beaconsfield [Disraeli] and Mr Gladstone are men of extraordinary ability; they dislike each other more than is usual among public men.' (*The Letters of Queen Victoria*, 2nd Series).

A similar view was expressed by Henry Locke in a letter to Lord Lytton in India on 21 November 1878: 'I have never known such strong feeling to exist on any question as on this [Afghanistan] and the Turkish question—friends of years standing become bitter foes —members of the same family don't speak one to the other—and when the questions are discussed, which they are morning noon and night by all classes and by both sexes there is an intensity of excitement that frequently breaks out into the most violent language—and it is all *purely personal*, the divergence of opinion not being so much upon the merits of the questions which seem seldom understood, but upon the feelings that are entertained either towards Lord Beaconsfield or Mr Gladstone.' (India Office Library, Letters from England).

An entry in Gladstone's diary 24 February, 1878 shows how high political feeling could run: 'Between four and six, three parties of the populace arrived here, the first with cheers, the two others hostile. Windows were broken and much hooting. The last detachment was only kept away by mounted police in line across the street both ways. ... There is strange work behind the curtain, if one could only get at it. The instigators are those really guilty; no one can wonder at the tools.'

And here is a riddle that was popular amongst the Tories in 1867: 'Why is Gladstone like a telescope? Because Disraeli draws him out, looks through him, and shuts him up.'

William Ewart Gladstone
William Ewart Gladstone was born on 29 December 1809, in Liverpool, where his father, a Scot, was a wealthy merchant. The Gladstones were active in local politics and played a leading part in securing the election of George Canning as Liverpool's Tory MP in 1812.

Gladstone's recollection of his first political part, at the age of

The house in Rodney Street, Liverpool, where Gladstone was born

three years old, was later published in *The Hawarden Papers*:
'My next recollection belongs to the period of Mr Canning's first
election for Liverpool, in the month of October of the year 1812.
Much entertaining went on in my father's house, where Mr
Canning himself was a guest; and on a day of a great dinner I was
taken down to the dining room. I was set upon one of the chairs,
standing, and directed to say to the company, "Ladies and
gentlemen".'

Gladstone was proud of his Scottish blood. In a speech he gave
in Dundee on 29 October 1890 he said: 'I am not slow to claim the
name of Scotsman, and even if I were, there is the fact staring me
in the face that not a drop of blood runs in my veins except what is
derived from a Scottish ancestry.'

13

In September 1821, the young Gladstone was sent to Eton, where he remained for six years. 'My tutor was the Rev. H. H. Knapp (practically all tutors were clergymen in those days). He was a reputed whig, an easy and kind-tempered man with a sense of scholarship, but no power of discipline, and no energy of desire to impress himself upon pupils ... I was placed in the middle remove fourth form, a place slightly better than the common run, but inferior to what a boy of good preparation or real excellence would have taken ...

'At this time there was not in me any desire to know or to excel. My first pursuits were football and then cricket; the first I did not long pursue, and in the second I never managed to rise above mediocrity and what was termed "the twenty-two".

'There was a barrister named Henry Hall Joy, a connection of my father through his first wife, and a man who had taken a first-class at Oxford. He was very kind to me, and had made some efforts to inspire me with a love of books, if not of knowledge. Indeed I had read Froissart, and Hume with Smollett, but only for the battles, and always skipping when I came to the sections headed "A Parliament". Joy had a taste for classics, and made visions for me of honours at Oxford. But the subject only danced before my eyes as a will-of-the-wisp, and without attracting me. I remained stagnant without heart or hope.

'A change, however, arrived about Easter 1822. My "remove" was then under Hawtrey (afterwards headmaster and provost), who was always on the lookout for any bud which he could warm with a little sunshine.' (*The Life of William Ewart Gladstone*, by John Morley.)

Years later, at a speech at Marlborough on the 3 February 1877, he commented: 'When I was at Eton, we knew very little indeed, but we knew it accurately.'

In his *Gleanings* (1878) he remembered, 'At Eton the actual teaching of Christianity was all but dead, though happily none of its forms had been surrendered.'

Gladstone left Eton in 1827 and went up to Oxford the following year. His college, Christ Church, whose members came mostly from the aristocracy, had a reputation for producing politicians; about half of Britain's prime ministers during the nineteenth

The schoolroom at Eton College where Gladstone studied as a boy

century were former students. Gladstone's own interest in politics grew while he was there, and he took part in many debates of the Oxford Union.

At one such debate, in May 1831, he spoke against the Reform Bill which had been laid before Parliament. During the general election of that year, he worked for the return of an anti-reform candidate.

Here is Gladstone's account of the debate of May 1831, quoted by Morley: 'There had never been anything like it known here before and will scarcely be again. The discussion on the question that the ministers were incompetent to carry on the government of the country was of a miscellaneous character, and I moved what they called a "rider" to the effect that the Reform bill threatened to change the form of British government, and ultimately to break up the whole frame of society.

'The debate altogether lasted three nights, and it closed then, partly because the *votes* had got tired of dancing attendance, partly because the speakers of the revolutionary side were exhausted. There were eight or nine more on ours ready, and indeed anxious. As it was, there were I think fifteen speeches on our side and thirteen on theirs, or something of that kind.

'Every man spoke above his average, and many very far beyond it. They were generally short enough. Moncreiff, a long-winded Scotsman, spouted nearly an hour, and I was guilty of three-quarters ... the division was favourable beyond anything we had hoped—ninety-four to thirty-eight.'

'I mounted the mare to join the anti-reform procession,' wrote Gladstone to his father, 'and we looked as well as we could do, considering that we were all covered with mud from head to foot. There was mob enough on both sides, but I must do them justice to say they were for the most part exceedingly good-humoured, and after we had dismounted, we went among them and elbowed one another and bawled and bellowed with the most perfect good temper. At the nomination in the town hall there was so much row raised that not one of the candidates could be heard.' The effect of all this, apparently, was to render Gladstone hoarse, and give him a chill.

Gladstone was rapidly becoming more and more involved in politics. He wrote in his Diary on 29 December 1831: 'This has been my debating society year, now, I fancy, done with. Politics are fascinating to me; perhaps too fascinating.'

Benjamin Disraeli Benjamin Disraeli was born in London on 21 December 1804. Unlike Gladstone and most other British statesmen of the nineteenth century, he attended neither public school nor university. It was not that the Disraeli family was poor. His father could afford to devote himself to literary studies, and both his younger brothers were sent to Winchester. Oxford and Cambridge still closed their doors to those who practised the Jewish religion—a restriction which lasted until 1858—but this would not have handicapped Disraeli, for he was baptised into the Christian faith when he was twelve.

Perhaps, as with his hero Vivian Grey, it was his mother who shaped the course of his education. In *Vivian Grey* (1826) Disraeli wrote: 'Mr Grey was for Eton but his lady was one of those women whom nothing in the world can persuade that a public school is anything but a place where boys are roasted alive; and so with tears, taunts, and supplications, the point of private education was conceded.'

Disraeli's schooldays He first attended a dame's school, and then a boarding-school at Blackheath. Many years later, two fellow pupils at Blackheath

The dining hall of Gladstone's Oxford College, Christ Church, in 1842

remembered their famous companion. On 28 April 1887 the Rev. E. Jones wrote in *The Standard*: 'He was a very rapid reader, was fond of romances, and would often let me sit by him and read the same book, good-naturedly waiting before turning a leaf till he knew I had reached the bottom of the page. He was very fond of playing at horses, and would often drive me and another boy as a pair with string reins. He was always full of fun; and at Midsummer, when he went home for the holidays in the basket of the Blackheath coach, fired away at the passers-by with his peashooter.'

And the *Jewish Chronicle* reported on 29 May 1868: '[Disraeli was] a lazy boy who excelled in none of the school exercises. However, he would amuse his companions on a wet half-holiday with a little extemporised drama. Being able to draw he would also construct a castle in paper as the scene of the adventures which he described. He had a taste not uncommon among schoolboys for little acts of bargaining and merchandise.'

From Blackheath Disraeli moved to Higham Hall, a school in Epping Forest, run by a Unitarian minister, the Reverend Eli Cogan. Disraeli recalled: 'I was thirteen, or about to be thirteen, when I went to him [Cogan], at Higham Hall, an old manor house, about two miles from Walthamstow. Nothing was thought of there but the two dead languages, but he was an admirable instructor in them as well as a first rate scholar.

Disraeli the fashionable author, drawn soon after the publication of
Vivian Grey

Fit for
University

'I ... was quite fit to have gone to a University when I left Cogan —I mean I did not require any preliminary cramming at a private tutor's. Not that I was more advanced than other boys of my age: not so advanced, and never could reach the first class, which consisted once of only one boy, Stratton, afterwards at Trinity College, Cambridge, and who, it was supposed, was to have carried everything before him there, and everywhere else, but I never heard of him since ...

'However, though I never reached the first class, and was not eminent even in the second, I learnt, or rather read a great deal in those years.'

Disraeli did not go to university. What, then, was he to do?

A year or more after leaving school Disraeli was articled to a firm of London solicitors. For this, his father had to pay a premium of 400 guineas, quite usual in those days. The work, however, was not to the young clerk's liking and he found the prospect of a legal career more and more unattractive. 'It would be a mistake to suppose that the two years and more that I was in the office of our friend were wasted. I have often thought, though I have often regretted the University, that it was much the reverse. My business was to be the private secretary of the busiest partner of our friend. He dictated to me every day his correspondence, which was as extensive as a Minister's, and when the clients arrived I did not leave the room, but remained not only to learn my business but to become acquainted with my future clients. They were in general men of great importance—bank directors, East India directors, merchants, bankers ... It gave me great facility with my pen and no inconsiderable knowledge of human nature ...

Disraeli the articled clerk

'I passed my evenings at home, alone, and always in deep study. This developed at last different feelings and views to those which I had willingly but too quickly adopted when I was little more than seventeen. I became pensive and restless, and before I was twenty I was obliged to terminate the dream of my father and his friend. Nothing would satisfy me but travel. My father then made a feeble effort for Oxford, but the hour of adventure had arrived. I was unmanageable.' (Quoted by Monypenny and G. E. Buckle.)

Disraeli travelled in Europe. Upon his return to London he tried to get rich quickly, first by speculating on the Stock Exchange (with disastrous results) then by attempting to launch a daily newspaper. This failed too. Finally, he wrote a novel, for which he received an initial payment of £200.

Seeking fortune

A letter written on the 3 October 1825 by a lawyer to Mr J. G. Lockhart, who had been offered the editorship of the proposed newspaper, states: 'Disraeli who is with you I have not seen much of, but I believe he is a sensible clever young fellow; his judgement however wants sobering down; he has never had to struggle with a single difficulty nor to act in any affairs in which his mind has necessarily been called on to consider and choose in difficult situations. At present his chief exertions as to matters of decision have been with regard to the selection of his food, his employment, and his clothing and, though he is honest and, I take it, wiser than his father, he is inexperienced and untried in the world, and of course, though you may, I believe, safely trust to his integrity, you cannot prudently trust much to his judgment.'

Disraeli as novelist Here is an echo from Disraeli's novel, *Vivian Grey*. 'Here dashed by the gorgeous equipage of Mrs Ormolu, the wife of a man who was working all the gold and silver mines in Christendom. "Ah! my dear Vivian," said Mr Grey, "it is *this* which has turned all your brains ... This thirst for sudden wealth it is, which engenders the extravagant conceptions, and fosters that wild spirit of speculation which is now stalking abroad ... Oh, my son, the wisest has said, 'He that maketh haste to be rich shall not be innocent' ".'

Vivian Grey appeared in 1826. Although the name of its author was concealed from the public, the publisher let it be known that he was a man who was familiar with the secrets of high society. Years later, Disraeli was ashamed of the book and called it 'a juvenile indiscretion'. At the time, however, its success encouraged him to write further novels. These tell us much about their author's beliefs and ambitions.

In *Contarini Fleming* (1832), written when he was twenty-eight, Disraeli asked: 'What were all those great poets of whom we now talk so much, what were they in their lifetime? The most miserable of their species ... A man of great energies aspires that they should be felt in his lifetime, that his existence should be rendered more intensely vital by the constant consciousness of his multiplied and multiplying power. Is posthumous fame a substitute for all this? ... We are active beings, and our sympathy above all other sympathies is with great action.'

Coningsby His political interests were often expressed. In *Coningsby* (1844) he wrote: 'Coningsby liked very much to talk politics with Millbank. He heard things from Millbank which were new to him ... he heard for the first time of influential classes in the country, who were not noble, and yet were determined to acquire power.'

' "Ancient lineage!" said Mr Millbank; "I never heard of a peer with an ancient lineage. The real old families of this country are to be found among the peasantry; the gentry, too, may lay some claim to old blood ... But a peer with an ancient lineage is to me quite a novelty".'

Later in the book:

' "I am sorry," said Coningsby rather pale, but speaking with firmness, "I am sorry that I could not support the Conservative party."

"By ——!" exclaimed Lord Monmouth starting in his seat, "some woman has got hold of him and made him a Whig!"

"No, my dear grandfather," said Coningsby scarcely able to repress a smile, serious as the interview was becoming, "nothing of the kind, I assure you. No person can be more anti-Whig."

"I don't know what you are driving at, sir," said Lord Monmouth in a hard, dry tone.

"I wish to be frank, sir," said Coningsby, "I have for a long time looked upon the Conservative party as a body who have betrayed their trust".'

Disraeli knew what it was like to lack money. He wrote feelingly in *Tancred* (1847): 'The two greatest stimulants in the world, Youth and Debt! What should I be without my debts, dear companions of my life that never desert me.'

In *Sybil* (1845), he spoke of the need for a new kind of Toryism: *Echo of* 'Toryism will yet rise from the tomb over which Bolingbroke shed *the future* his last tear, to bring back strength to the Crown, liberty to the Subject, and to announce that power has only one duty: to secure the social welfare of the *people*.'

Something of Disraeli's own ambitions are reflected in *Contarini Fleming*: 'I heard my name. The hall was now darkened. In the distance stood my father. I joined him. I placed his arm affectionately in mine, and said to me, "My son, you will be Prime Minister of ——; perhaps something greater." '

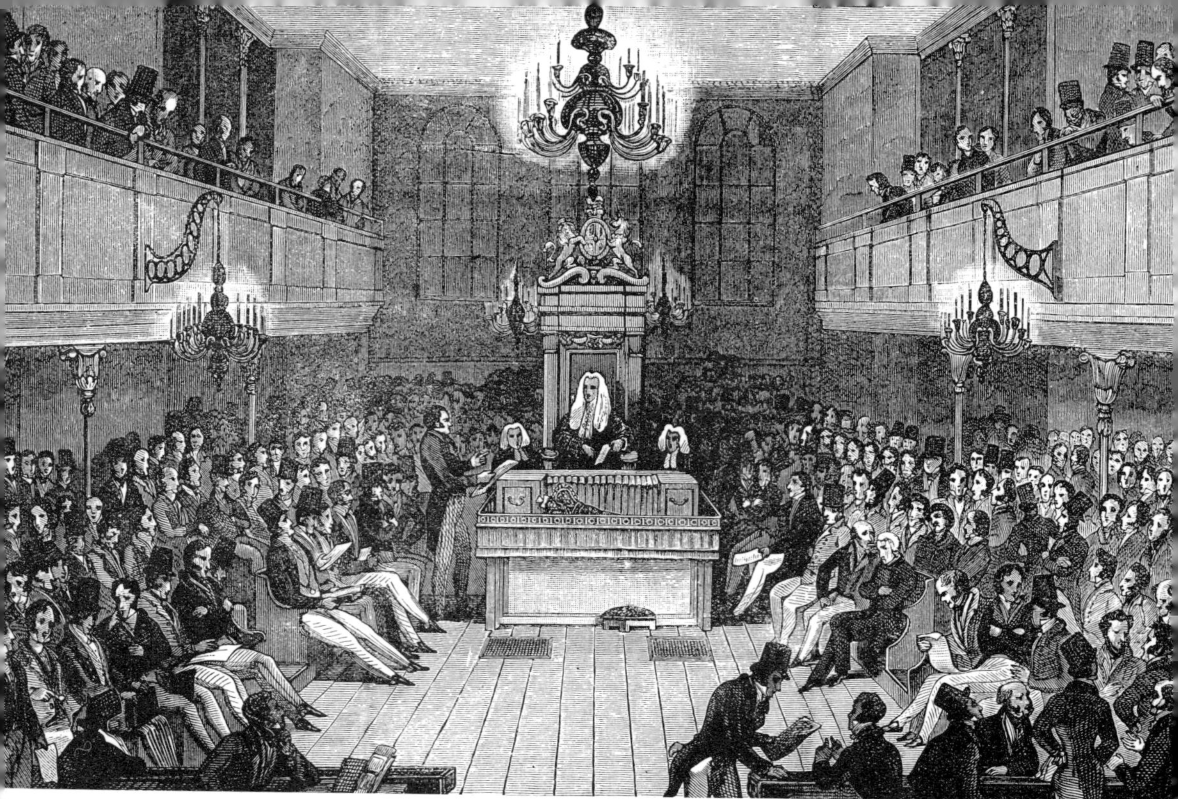

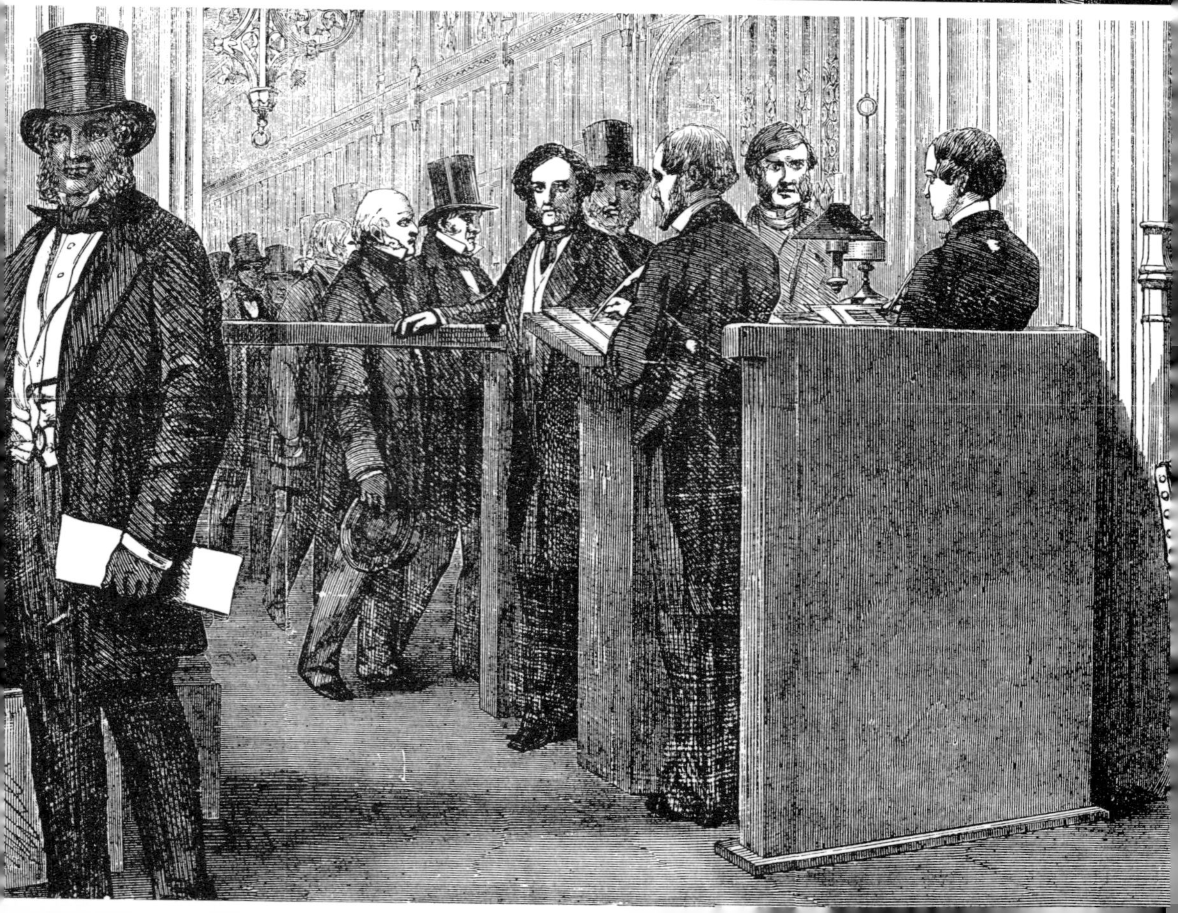

2 New Members

GLADSTONE AND DISRAELI first entered Parliament during the 1830s. Although the Reform Act had enlarged the electorate and had brought about some redistribution of seats, it disappointed many of its supporters. Many constituencies were still left in the control of powerful landowners. The Act did little to check corruption at election times, and nothing was done to introduce the secret ballot, which many people called for.

The Reform Act, which was passed by Parliament on 7 June 1832, gave the vote to the wealthy middle class. It created new constituencies (like Salford, Tynemouth and Merthyr Tydvil) and ended the life of many others, which were considered to be 'rotten boroughs' (like Old Sarum, Winchelsea and Ilchester). It did not, however, greatly affect the membership of Parliament, as those who sat in the House of Commons, whether Whigs or Tories, were still mainly drawn from the aristocracy.

Becoming a Member of Parliament

'... It is expedient to take effectual measures for correcting divers abuses that have long prevailed in the choice of members to serve in the commons house of parliament, to deprive many inconsiderable places of the right of returning members, to grant such privilege to large, populous and wealthy towns, to increase the franchise of the knights of the shire, to extend the electors' franchise to many of His Majesty's subjects who have not heretofore enjoyed the same, and to diminish the expense of elections.'

In 1832 both Gladstone and Disraeli took part in their first parliamentary contests. Gladstone, only a few months after leaving Oxford, was invited to fight as a Tory for one of the two seats at Newark, a constituency in which the Duke of Newcastle had great

Gladstone on the hustings

23

Facing page: above Inside the House of Commons (1834), with the Speaker in the centre. *Below* Members of Parliament voting in the Division Lobby

influence. There were three candidates: Gladstone polled 887 votes, his fellow Tory 798, and the unsuccessful Whig 726. He was in.

Here is part of Gladstone's speech to the constituents of Newark on the 12 December 1832, after the result of the poll: 'Gentlemen; in looking forward to the field which is now opened before me, I cannot but conceive that I shall often be reproached with being not your representative but the representative of the Duke of Newcastle ... I met the Duke of Newcastle upon the broad ground of principle, and upon that ground alone. I own no other bond of union with him than this, that he in his exalted sphere, and I in my humble one, entertained the same persuasion, that the institutions of this country are to be defended against those who threaten their destruction ...

'Why do you return me to parliament? Not because I am the Duke of Newcastle's man, simply: but because, coinciding with the duke in political sentiment, you likewise admit that one possessing so large a property here, and faithfully discharging the duties which the possession of that property entails, ought in the natural course of things to exercise a certain influence.'

Towards the end of his life, Gladstone recounted his feelings on taking up his first parliamentary seat: 'I took my seat at the opening of 1833, provided unquestionably with a large stock of schoolboy bashfulness. The first time that business required me to go to the arm of the chair to say something to the Speaker ... I remember the revival in me bodily of the frame of mind in which a schoolboy stands before his master. But apart from an incidental recollection of this kind, I found it most difficult to believe with any reality of belief, that such a poor and insignificant creature as I, could really belong to, really form a *part* of, an assembly which, notwithstanding the prosaic character of its entire visible equipment, I felt to be so august.'

Fifth time lucky! Disraeli found it very much harder to enter Parliament. Standing as a Radical at High Wycombe, he twice fought unsuccessful elections during 1832. In June, when only the Corporation and burgesses were allowed to vote—he lost by 20 votes to 12—and again in December when, with a reformed electorate, he polled 119 against his opponents' 179 and 140.

24

Gladstone (*right*) and Disraeli (*left*) who between them dominated English politics during the second part of the nineteenth century

In a letter to Benjamin Austin, dated June 1832, Disraeli wrote: 'I start on the high Radical interest ... Toryism is worn out, and I cannot condescend to be a Whig.'

At first, surprise was shown at Disraeli's ability to capture the interest of a crowd. 'Tales are still told in Wycombe of that famous first speech from the portico of the *Red Lion*. The youthful orator was now at the height of his dandyism, and his 'curls and ruffles' played no small part in the election. Standing on the top of the porch beside the figure of the lion, with his pale face set off by masses of jet-black hair and his person plenteously adorned with lace and cambric, he must have seemed to the spectators better fitted for the role of fashionable novelist than for that of strenuous politician. Great, then, was their surprise when this 'popinjay', as a hostile newspaper called him, began to pour forth a torrent of eloquence with tremendous energy of action and in a voice that carried far along the High Street. He had an instinct for the dramatic effects which hold the attention of a mob.' (Quoted by Monypenny and Buckle.)

Disraeli becomes a Tory

By 1835 Disraeli had become a Tory, believing that the party was now more progressive than it had been. That year he made two further attempts to win a parliamentary seat, at High Wycombe (for the third time), then at Taunton. But still he failed.

Yet Disraeli would not let himself be deterred by his defeat at High Wycombe. In a speech at a Conservative dinner he said: 'I am not at all disheartened. I do not in any way feel like a beaten man. Perhaps it is because I am used to it. I will say of myself like the famous Italian general, who being asked in his old age why he was always victorious, replied, it was because he had always been beaten in his youth.'

Success and failure

Not until July 1837 were his efforts at last rewarded. On 30 June 1837, Disraeli wrote to his sister, Sarah, full of enthusiasm: 'The clouds have at length dispelled, and my prospects seem as bright as the day. At six o'clock this evening I start for Maidstone with Wyndham Lewis[1], and I suppose by Wednesday I shall have completed my canvass. I doubt whether there will be a contest.'

He wrote again on 4 July: 'Last night there was a full meeting, and I think I made the best speech I ever made yet ... I do not see how we can be defeated.'

Sarah Disraeli received a terse but jubilant note from him on 27 July: 'Dearest, Lewis 707, Disraeli 616, Colonel Thompson 412. The constituency nearly exhausted. In haste, Dizzy.'

On 15 November 1837, Disraeli wrote to Sarah of mounting tension and excitement: 'I took my seat this morning: I went down to the House with Wyndham at two, and found it very full, the members standing in groups and chatting. About three, there was a cry of "Order, order," all took their seats (myself on the second bench behind Sir Robert Peel), and a messenger summoned the Commons. The Government party was very strong in consequence of an article in *The Times*[2] about two days back ... Peel said a very little, very well. Then Abercromby [the Speaker], who looked like an old laundress, mumbled and moaned some dullness, and was then carried to the chair, and said a little more amid a faint, dull cheer. To me of course the scene was exciting enough, but none could share my feelings except new members.'

[1] The borough of Maidstone returned two members to Parliament. Wyndham Lewis, who had already been an MP, was the other Tory candidate.

[2] This hinted that the Tories were planning to oppose the re-election of Abercromby as Speaker.

Unfortunately, however, his mood was soon to change. He wrote to Sarah again on 8 December 1837: 'I made my maiden speech last night, rising very late after O'Connell, but at the re- quest of my party and the full sanction of Sir Robert Peel. As I wish to give you an exact idea of what occurred, I state at once that my *début* was a *failure*.'

On the same day the *Morning Chronicle* quoted the speech: ' "When we remember at the same time that, with emancipated Ireland and enslaved England, on the one hand a triumphant nation, on the other a groaning people, and notwithstanding the noble lord, secure on the pedestal of power, may wield in one hand the keys of St Peter, and" —— (Here the Hon. Member was interrupted with such loud and incessant bursts of laughter that it was impossible to know whether he really closed his sentence or not). The Hon. Member concluded in these words: "Now, Mr Speaker, we see the philosophical prejudices of man." (Laughter and cheers.) "I respect cheers, even when they come from the lips of political opponents." (Renewed laughter) "I think, sir ——" (Hear, hear, and repeated cries of "Question, question.") "I am not at all surprised, sir, at the reception which I have received." (Continued laughter.) "I have begun several times many things ——" (laughter) "—— and I have often succeeded at last." (Fresh cries of, "Question!") "Ay, sir, and though I sit down now, the time will come when you will hear me!" The Hon. Member de- livered the last sentence in a very loud tone, and resumed his seat.'

Gladstone had made his maiden speech some four years before, during a debate on the Whig Government's Bill to end slavery in the Empire. Gladstone's father, an absentee West Indian planta- tion owner, was one of those accused of ill-treating their slaves. The new MP denied the charge. He agreed that slaves should be set free, but not until they had become Christians. So he opposed the Bill.

Morley described Gladstone's speech: 'The speech was an un- common success. Stanley, the minister mainly concerned, con- gratulated him with more than those conventional compliments which the good nature of the House of Commons expects to be paid to any decent beginner. "I never listened to any speech with

greater pleasure"; said Stanley, himself the prince of debators and then in the most brilliant part of his career, "the member for Newark argued his case with a temper, an ability, and a fairness which may well be cited as a good model to many older members of this House." His own leader, though he spoke later, said nothing in his speech about the new recruit, but two days after Mr Gladstone mentioned that Sir R. Peel came up to him and praised Monday night's affair. King William wrote to Althorp: "he rejoices that a young member has come forward in so promising a manner, as Viscount Althorp states Mr W. E. Gladstone to have done." '

In December 1834, Whig rule came to an end and for a few months Peel was Prime Minister at the head of a minority Tory Government. Gladstone, who was just twenty-five, was given a junior post at the Treasury. His diary shows some difficulties of travel at this time: 'December 17. Went to meet the post, found a letter from Peel desiring to see me, dated 13th. All haste; ready by 4—no place! Reluctantly deferred till the morning. Wrote to Lincoln, Sir R. Peel, etc. ... A game of whist. This is a serious call. I got my father's advice to take anything with work and responsibility. 18th: off at 7.40 by mail. I find it a privation to be unable to read in a coach. The mind is distracted through the senses, and rambles. Nowhere is it to me so incapable of continuous thought ... Newcastle at $9\frac{1}{4}$ p.m. 19th: same again. At York $6\frac{1}{4}$ a.m. to 7. Ran to peep at the minster and bore away a faint twilight image of its grandeur. 20th: arrived safe, thank God, and well at the Bull and Mouth $5\frac{3}{4}$ a.m. Albany soon. To bed for $2\frac{1}{4}$ hours. Went to Peel about eleven.'

Gladstone's first post

Opposite Disraeli's maiden speech to the House of Commons on 8 December 1837 was a complete disaster. Laughed down by the other members he retired, promising that one day they would have to listen

3 Rising Stars

IN 1815, at the end of the war with Napoleon, an Act was passed prohibiting the importation of foreign corn until the home price had reached 80s a quarter. This law, with some modifications, remained in operation until 1846. It became a focus of the struggle which developed between the protectionists, and those who favoured a system of free trade.

Gladstone, who had supported protection, began to change his views. Disraeli, however, had no doubts. He was one of a small aristocratic group which called itself 'Young England'. Its members were anxious to strengthen the Crown and the Anglican Church. They believed in a benevolent approach to the working-classes and were strongly opposed to free trade.

Protection or free trade? Following the general election of 1835, Gladstone was once more in Opposition, where he stayed until 1841. In that year, when Peel and the Conservatives (Tories) came to power, he was appointed Vice-President of the Board of Trade.

Britain was in a state of unrest. The Chartist movement, with its demands for parliamentary reforms, was gathering strength. Unemployment was widespread. Harsh working conditions were to be found in mines and factories, and there was fierce opposition to the new Poor Law which had been introduced in 1834. Many people believed that the country's economic difficulties were caused by the protective barriers which had been set up against imports. In particular, these free traders wanted to scrap the Corn Laws, and gave their support to the Anti-Corn Law League formed by Cobden and Bright. Gladstone, a lifelong protectionist, gradually modified his views.

Towards the end of his life, Gladstone recalled: 'When I entered parliament in 1832, the great controversy between protection or artificial restraint and free trade, of which Cobden was the leading figure, did not enter into the popular controversies of the day, and was still in the hands of the philosophers. My father was an active and effective local politician. Protectionism ... I inherited from him and from all my youthful associations ... Moreover, for the first six years or so of my parliamentary life free trade was in no way a party question, and it only became strictly such in 1841 ... In 1833 only, the question was debated in the House of Commons,

The Chartists' mass march to Kennington in 1848

and the speech of the mover against the corn laws made me uncomfortable. But the reply of Sir James Graham restored my peace of mind ...

He added 'On the change of Government, Peel, with much judgment, offered me the Vice-Presidentship of the Board of

31

Trade. On sound principles of party discipline, I took the office at once; and having taken it I set to work with all my might as a worker ... And now the stones of which my protectionism was built began to get uncomfortably loose. When we came to the question of tariff, we were all nearly on a par in ignorance, and we had a very bad adviser in Macgregor, secretary to the Board of Trade. But I had the advantage of being able to apply myself with an undivided attention. My assumption of office at the Board of Trade was followed by hard, steady, and honest work; and every day so spent beat like a battering ram on the unsure fabric of my official protectionism.'

Peel's Government In a letter written to Queen Victoria in 1880, Gladstone praised Peel: 'In many of the most important rules of public policy Sir R. Peel's government surpassed generally the governments which have succeeded it, whether liberal or conservative. Among them I would mention purity in patronage, financial strictness, loyal adherence to the principle of public economy, jealous regard to the rights of parliament, a single eye to the public interest, strong aversion to extension of territorial responsibilities and a frank admission of the rights of foreign countries as equal to those of their own.'

Amongst the measures passed by Peel's government was a Railway Act (1844), for which Gladstone was responsible. This brought in regulations to control the rapidly growing railways and gave the state power to take them over if necessary.

Despite its good record, however, many Conservatives began to

A Protectionist meeting ends in noisy disorder (Lincoln, 1850)

Cartoon showing Cobden, the Free-Trader and Corn Law abolitionist,
leading Robert Peel, the Prime Minister, towards these aims faster than
he wishes to go

distrust Peel's leadership. His policies, whether relating to
Catholicism, Irish nationalism or economic matters, seemed
much too liberal. Disraeli was one of Peel's most severe critics.
Peel, he said, had too much in common with the Whigs.

On 1 March 1845, Disraeli wrote to *The Times*: '[Peel] may *Disraeli and*
object to me, although I think he has no great occasion to object *Peel*
that I am sometimes in a different lobby to himself; but I was sent
to swell a Tory majority—to support a Tory Ministry. Whether a
Tory Ministry exists or not I do not pretend to decide; but I am

33

C

bound to believe that the Tory majority still remains, and therefore I do not think that it is the majority that should cross the
House, but only the Ministry.'

Irish famine   A crisis arose late in 1845. Failure of the Irish potato crop,
destroyed by blight, threatened Ireland with famine. Peel had so

Sir Robert Peel: under his able leadership the Tories became a
reforming, progressive party

far refused to abolish the Corn Laws from fear of splitting his
party—many Tories were landowners who demanded the protection of agriculture. But he now decided to risk a revolt amongst
his supporters.

Gladstone many years later reflected: 'I think he [Peel] expected
to carry the repeal of the corn law without breaking up his party,
but meant at all hazard to carry it.'

Lord Aberdeen also commented on the situation (quoted in Mrs
Simpson's *Many Memories*): 'With the exception of Graham and

myself, his whole cabinet was against him. Lyndhurst, Goulburn, and Stanley were almost violent in their resistance. Still more opposed to him, if it were possible, was the Duke of Wellington. To break up the cabinet was an act of great courage.'

On 16 February 1846, Peel made a speech on the Second Reading of the Bill for the Repeal of the Corn Laws: 'While I retained the hope of acting with a united Administration, while I thought there was a prospect of bringing this question to a settlement, I determined to retain office and incur its responsibilities. When I was compelled to abandon that hope ... I took the earliest opportunity, consistent with a sense of duty and of public honour, of tendering my resignation to the Queen.'

Who would form a new government? Lord John Russell, the Whig leader, tried, but with no success. Disraeli, who was staying in Paris, thought that Gladstone might have a chance. Here is a letter he wrote to Lord John Manner on 17 December 1845: 'I heard last night from a good quarter that the Whigs had resolved to decline the enterprise. The King [of France] inquired whether Gladstone ... could not lead the *personnel* of the Commons, with the Duke in the Lords ...

'The King inquired a great deal about Gladstone of me. It was evident that his name had recently been suggested to His Majesty by some high quarter. I told the King that he was quite equal to Peel, with the advantage of youth.'

But Gladstone's day was yet to come. Peel returned to office with a new Cabinet which was agreed about the need to free the trade in corn.

On the Second Reading of the Bill to Repeal the Corn Laws, *Repeal of* given on 16 February, 1846, Sir Robert Peel told the House: 'This *Corn Laws* night is to decide between the policy of continued relaxation of restriction, or the return to restraint and prohibition. This night you will select the motto which is to indicate the commercial policy of England. Shall it be "advance" or "recede"? Which is to be the fitter motto for this great Empire?'

He went on to say: 'We have an extent of coast greater in proportion to our population and the area of our land than any other great nation securing to us maritime strength and superiority. Iron and coal, the sinews of manufacture, give us advantages

over every other rival in the great competition of industry. Our capital far exceeds that which they can command. In ingenuity—in skill—in energy—we are inferior to none. Our national character, the free institutions under which we live, the liberty of thought and action, an unshackled press, spreading the knowledge of every discovery and of every advance in science—combine with our natural and physical advantages to place us at the head of these nations which profit by the free interchange of their products.

'And,' he asked, 'is this the country to shrink from competition? Is this the country to adopt a retrograde policy? Is this the country which can flourish in the sickly artificial atmosphere of prohibition? Is this the country to stand shivering on the brink of exposure to the healthful breezes of competition?'

During the Third Reading of the Bill, on 15 May 1846, Disraeli accused Peel of deceiving his Party: 'If we think the opinions of the Anti-Corn Law League are dangerous ... it is open in a free country like England for men who hold opposite views to resist them with the same earnestness, by all legitimate means ... But what happens in this country? A body of gentlemen, able and adroit men, come forward, and profess contrary doctrines to those of these new economists. They place themselves at the head of that great popular party who are adverse to the new ideas, and, professing their opinions, they climb and clamber into power by having accepted, or rather by having eagerly sought the trust.'

He added, 'we trusted to others—to one who by accepting, or rather by seizing that post, obtained the greatest place in the country, and at this moment governs England ... I think the right Hon. Baronet may congratulate himself on his complete success in having entirely deceived his party.'

The Bill to repeal the Corn Laws was passed because the Opposition supported the Government. Most Conservatives, including Disraeli, voted against it.

The Conservatives split

Gladstone had no seat in the House at the time, as he had just been appointed Secretary of State for War and Colonies. During the nineteenth century, ministers on appointment had to seek re-election to the Commons. Generally, this created few difficulties for a new minister. However, Gladstone found that the Duke of

Opposite Peel announces his adoption of the principles of free trade during the Corn Law debate in the Commons (January, 1846)

Newcastle, a staunch protectionist, was no longer willing to use his influence at Newark on behalf of a 'Peelite'. Not until August 1847 did Gladstone re-enter Parliament as MP for Oxford University.

Once the Corn Laws had been abolished, Peel could no longer command the support of the House. Russell formed a Whig Government and with the help of the Peelite Conservatives, stayed

Disraeli speaking at the Bucks election in 1847

in power for the next six years. Disraeli became a prominent figure amongst those Conservatives who remained in opposition.

In his book *Lord George Bentinck* (1851), Disraeli spoke with respect of Peel: 'This remarkable man, who in private life was constrained and often awkward, who could never address a public meeting or make an after-dinner speech without being ill at ease, and generally saying something stilted or even a little ridiculous, in the senate was the readiest, easiest, most flexible and adroit of

38

men. He played upon the House of Commons as on an old fiddle.'

On 25 March 1847, B. E. Lindo wrote in a letter to Sarah Disraeli: 'I was very charmed with Dizzy's display last Tuesday, and astonished at the command and control of the House which he possesses—the buzz everywhere in the lobbies and galleries when he rose, and the rush into the House, which filled in no time after he had begun. In every way I was astonished and pleased ... Dizzy's figure suits the floor of the House admirably, while his voice is so various, modulated musically at one moment and pouring out its thunder the next, and you hear plainly every whisper. He extracted cheers from a full House of opponents. What would they have been if they had gone with him! He certainly is the wonder of the day, and begins to be universally acknowledged so.'

Gladstone's New Seat

Gladstone later wrote: 'I remained without a seat until the dissolution in June 1847. But several months before this occurred it had become known that Mr Estcourt would vacate his seat for Oxford, and I became a candidate. It was a serious campaign. The constituency, much to its honour, did not stoop to fight the battle on the ground of protection. But it was fought, and that fiercely, on religious grounds ... The upshot was favourable. The liberals supported me gallantly, so did many zealous churchmen, apart from politics, and a good number of moderate men, so that I was returned by a fair majority. I held the seat for eighteen years, but with five contests and a final defeat.'

Colonial affairs

Protection had been a great help to Britain's colonies. Colonial exports were allowed to come into this country on payment of lower tariffs than those from other countries. With free trade, a new colonial policy was needed—if the ties with many parts of her Empire were not to be endangered. The Whigs believed that the people living in these overseas territories should have a greater share in their government.

Gladstone, who regularly spoke on colonial affairs in the House, agreed.

But in a letter to Lord Malmesbury of 13 August 1852, Disraeli complained: 'Those wretched colonies will all be independent too in a few years and are a millstone round our necks.'

4 On the Front Bench

THE SECOND HALF of the nineteenth century began with a promise of brighter, more prosperous times ahead. Britain was firmly established as the 'workshop of the world', a position she was to maintain for the next twenty years. Chartism was dead, trade unionism was becoming more respectable, and social discontent was less marked than it had been in the thirties and forties. The various political groups that sat in Parliament were soon to re-form into two great parties which, together, dominated the political scene until the First World War. *Workshop of the world*

In 1852 Parliament contained no less than five main political groups. These were the Whigs, led by Russell and Palmerston; the Conservative Free Traders (Peelites), led by Aberdeen and Gladstone; Conservatives, who had until recently been protectionists, led by Lord Derby (formerly Edward Stanley) and Disraeli; the Radicals, led by Cobden and Bright; and the Irish. Consequently, government tended to be unstable. *Disraeli as Chancellor*

In February, Russell lost control of the Commons, largely due to a quarrel with Palmerston, and had to resign. The Queen invited Derby to form a government. With the Prime Minister in the Lords, Disraeli was now asked to lead the Lower House as Chancellor of the Exchequer. For many members of the new cabinet, including Disraeli, this was the first time that they had held ministerial office.

Speaking at a Royal Literary Fund Dinner on 13 May 1852, William Thackeray referred to Disraeli with great admiration: 'Could a romance writer in after-years have a better or more wondrous hero than that of an individual who at twenty years of *'A wondrous hero'*

Opposite left: top and below Bright and Cobden, leaders of the Radicals, *right top* Lord Palmerston with Russell (leader of the Commons) and *below* Prince Albert, Queen Victoria's Consort

C *

age wrote *Vivian Grey* and a little while afterwards *The Wondrous Tale of Alroy* ... who then went into politics, faced, fought, and conquered the great political giant of these days; and who subsequently led thanes and earls to battle, while he caused reluctant squires to carry his lance?'

'What a hero would not that be for some future novelist, and what a magnificent climax for the third volume of his story, when he led him, in his gold coat of office, to kiss the Queen's hand as the Chancellor of the Exchequer!'

A critical account of Disraeli's new appointment appeared in the *Edinburgh Review* (1853): 'His appointment to this post was one of the most startling domestic events which has occurred in our time. People seemed never tired of talking and speculating on it, with its recondite causes and its problematical results. He at once became an inexhaustible topic of animated discussion in society. His portrait was painted by one fashionable artist; his bust was taken in marble by another; what were called likenesses of him appeared in illustrated newspapers by the dozen; and above all, he was placed in Madame Tussaud's repository—that British Valhalla in which it is difficult for a civilian to gain a niche without being hanged. He glittered in the political horizon as a star of the first magnitude; and every glass was turned on him the more eagerly because it was impossible to discover and hazardous to predicate whether he would turn out a planet, a fixed star, a comet, or a mere vapoury exhalation, or will o' the wisp, raised by an overheated atmosphere from a rank and unwholesome soil.'

As the year drew to a close it was clear that the Government was *The* running into difficulties. In a letter to Lord Derby, dated 26 *December* November 1852, Prince Albert wrote: 'My conviction is now *Budget* further confirmed that Lord Palmerston is aiming at the leadership of the House of Commons, in order to possess himself of *absolute power*, and that he is taking his position in a way to obtain this, whether the debate may end in a junction of the Peelites with your Government or with Lord John Russell, whom he would in that case wish to see removed to the House of Lords ...'

The Prince suggested, 'Should Mr Disraeli have to relinquish the lead, Mr Gladstone would be a much fitter successor than Lord Palmerston, for, whatever his peculiar crotchets may be, he is a

Opposite Lord Stanley, later Lord Derby, Conservative leader in the House of Lords

man of the strictest feelings of honour and the purest mind.'

The end for Disraeli came in December when, after many days of debate on his budget proposals, the Conservatives were defeated by 305 to 286, the Whigs, Peelites, Radicals and Irish voting against.

Gladstone on Disraeli Gladstone recorded in his Diary on 18 December 1852: 'I have never gone through so exciting a passage of parliamentary life. The intense efforts which we made to obtain, and the Government to escape, a definite issue, were like a fox chase, and prepared us all for excitement. ... Disraeli rose at 10.20 [on 16 December], and from that moment, of course, I was on tenterhooks, except when his superlative acting and brilliant oratory from time to time absorbed me and made me quite *forget* that I had to follow him. He spoke until one.

'His speech as a whole was grand; I think the most powerful I ever heard from him. At the same time it was disgraced by shameless personalities and otherwise; I had therefore to begin by attacking him for these. There was a question whether it would not be too late, but when I heard his personalities I felt there was no choice but to go on.'

He added: 'My great object was to show the Conservative Party how their leader was hoodwinking and bewildering them, and this I have the happiness of believing that in some degree I effected; for while among some there was great heat and a disposition to interrupt me when they could, I could *see* in the faces and demeanour of others quite other feelings expressed. But it was a most difficult operation, and altogether it might have been better effected ... I am told he is much stung by what I said. I am very sorry it fell to me to say it; God knows I have no wish to give him pain; and really with my deep sense of his gifts I would only pray they might be well used.'

With no single party in Parliament strong enough to form a government, the Whigs and Aberdeen's Peelites tried a coalition. Gladstone took Disraeli's place as Chancellor of the Exchequer: many thought that this was appropriate, for 'Mr G. destroyed the budget, so he ought to make a new one.'

Gladstone resigns But it was foreign affairs, not economic policy, which dominated parliament. The Crimean War started in 1854. The first winter

Opposite top For a brief moment their dislike of the Crimean War and its conduct united Disraeli (*right*) and Gladstone (*left*) in common cause. *Below* Queen Victoria receives Crimea soldiers outside Buckingham Palace

brought near destruction to the British army and there was a public outcry over the way that the war was being mismanaged. The army lacked proper supplies and medical aid. The Aberdeen coalition collapsed, and was now replaced by a Ministry, mainly of Whigs, under Palmerston. Gladstone accepted an offer to join the Cabinet, but almost at once resigned.

He explained in his diary on 28 February 1855: 'This day at a quarter to three I attended at the palace to resign the seals, and had an audience of about twenty minutes. The Queen, in taking them over, was pleased to say that she received them with great pain. I answered that the decision which had required me to surrender them had been the most painful of my public life ... I trusted HM would believe that we [two other ministers had resigned at the same time] had all been governed by no other desire than to do what was best for the interests of the Crown and the country.

'HM expressed her confidence of this, and at no time throughout the conversation did she in any manner indicate an opinion that our decision had been wrong. She spoke of the difficulty of making arrangements for carrying on the Government in the present state of things, and I frankly gave my opinion to HM that she would have little peace or comfort in these matters, until Parliament should have returned to its old organisation in two political parties.

'That at present we were in a false position, and that both sides of the House were demoralised—the ministerial side overcharged with an excess of official men, and the way stopped up against expectants, which led to subdivision, jealousy, and intrigue; the opposition so weak in persons having experience of affairs ...'

Gladstone continued: 'HM seeming to agree in my main position, as did the Prince, asked me: "But when will parliament return to that state?" I replied I grieved to say that I perceived neither the time when, nor the manner how, that result is to come about; but until it is reached, I fear that YM will pass through a period of instability and weakness as respects the executive. She observed that the prospect is not agreeable. I said, True, madam, but it is a great consolation that all these troubles are upon the surface, and that the throne has for a long time been gaining and not losing stability from year to year.'

Whether in or out of office, Gladstone led a very full life. As a closing entry to his diary of the following year, he wrote: 'See how I stand. Into politics I am drawn deeper every year; in the growing anxieties and struggles of the church I have no less [interest] than I have heretofore; literature has of late acquired a new and powerful hold upon me; the fortunes of my wife's family, which have had, with all their dry detail, all the most exciting and arduous interest of romance for me during nine years and more; seven children growing up around us, and each day the object of deeper thoughts and feelings, and of higher hopes to Catherine [his wife] and me—what a network is here woven out of all that the heart and all that the mind of man can supply.'

Gladstone at home

Gladstone remained bitterly opposed to Palmerston. Anxious to bring about the downfall of the Government, he found himself battling alongside the Conservatives in the Commons and even, at times, planned tactics with Derby and Disraeli.

Gladstone and the Conservatives

In early February 1857, Gladstone recorded in his diary: 'This afternoon at three I called on Lord Derby and remained with him above three hours, in prosecution of the correspondence which had passed between us.

'I told him that I deliberately disapproved of the government of Lord Palmerston, and was prepared and desirous to aid in any proper measures which might lead to its displacement. That so strong were my objections that I was content to act thus without inquiring who was to follow, for I was convinced that any one who might follow would govern with less prejudice to public interests.'

Palmerston's policy in China came under attack when the Prime Minister approved of the bombardment of Canton by a naval squadron: this action was in retaliation for the seizure, by the Chinese authorities, of a ship which was flying the British flag. Both Gladstone and Disraeli spoke in the ensuing debate held in the House of Commons on 3 March 1857.

Gunboat diplomacy

Gladstone protested: 'War taken at the best is a frightful scourge upon the human race; but because it is so, the wisdom of ages has surrounded it with strict laws and usages, and has required formalities to be observed which shall act as a curb upon the wild passions of man ... You have dispensed with all these precautions.'

Disraeli agreed with this: 'We must habituate ourselves to the idea of extending to countries like China the same diplomatic intercourse that we adopt with other nations ... You are dealing with a country of immense antiquity. You have been reminded in the debate that China enjoys a civilisation of twenty-five centuries. In point of antiquity, the civilisation of Europe is nothing to that. But the result of those ancient habits and customs is an existence

Lord Palmerston, leader of the Whigs and bitter opponent of Gladstone

of profound ceremony and formal etiquette; and yet you expect that such a country will not be startled by the frank and occasionally, I am sorry to say, the brutal freedom of European manners.'

General Election (1857)

The vote went against the Government. Palmerston, confident of success in the country, resigned and put his trust in a general election. He won a resounding victory.

Disraeli was not too dismayed by the result. In a letter to Mrs Bridges Williams, dated 12 April 1857, he explained: 'I am by no means dissatisfied by the results of the General Election, strange and startling as they have been. They realise what I foretold: we shall now have a House of Commons with two parties and with definite opinions. All the sections, all the conceited individuals, who were what they styled themselves, "independent", have been swept away, erased, obliterated, expunged. The state of affairs will be much more wholesome, and more agreeable.

'The Conservative party have got through the ordeal very well. Though numerically a little lessened, they are much more compact and united, and even as regards numbers, when a due occasion offers, will bring a larger force into the field than in the last Parliament. Although we had then 280 and more on the muster-roll, still, when the hour of battle arrived, we never could count on more than 220, the rest absent, or worse, against us.'

Though Gladstone was sometimes ready to work with the Conservatives, he had no wish to make a permanent alliance with them. When, in February 1858, Palmerston was surprisingly defeated over a Conspiracy Bill, Gladstone refused to join the Conservative Ministry which Lord Derby had been invited to form. *Gladstone declines*

On 20 February 1858, Gladstone wrote in his diary: 'Palmerston has resigned. He is down. I must now cease to denounce him.'

The following day Gladstone received a letter from Lord Derby: 'In consequence of the adverse vote of the other night, in which you took so prominent and distinguished a part, the government, as you know, has resigned; and I have been entrusted by the Queen with the difficult task, which I have felt it my duty not to decline, of forming an administration. In doing so, I am very desirous, if possible, of obtaining the co-operation of men of eminence, who are not at this moment fettered by other ties, and whose principles are not incompatible with my own. Believing that you stand in this position, it would afford me very great satisfaction if I could obtain your valuable aid in forming my proposed cabinet.'

On the following day (21 February) John Bright also wrote to Gladstone: 'Will you forgive me if I write to you on this matter? I say nothing but in the most friendly spirit, and I have some confidence that you will not misinterpret what I am doing. Lord Derby has only about one-third of the House of Commons with him—and it is impossible by any management, or by dissolution, to convert this minority to a majority. His minority in the House is greater and more powerful than it is in the country ... the whole Liberal party in the country dislike him, and they dislike his former leader in the Commons ... If you join Lord Derby, you link your fortunes with a constant minority, and with a party in the country which is every day lessening in numbers and power. If you remain on our side of the House, you are with the majority, and no government can be formed without you ... I know nothing that can prevent your being Prime Minister before you approach the age of every other member of the House who has or can have any claim to that high office.' Gladstone, however, declined.

Disraeli appeals to Gladstone
So for the second time, Disraeli became Chancellor of the Exchequer under Derby's leadership. In May 1858 a vacancy in the Cabinet led him to write warmly to Gladstone, as Lord Derby had done before: 'I think it of ... paramount importance to the public interests that you should assume at this time a commanding position in the administration of affairs ... If you join Lord Derby's Cabinet, you will meet there some warm personal friends; all its members are your admirers. You may place me in neither category, but in that, I assure you, you have ever been sadly mistaken.

'The vacant post is, at this season, the most commanding in the Commonwealth; if it were not, whatever office you filled, your shining qualities would always render you supreme; and if party necessities retain me formally in the chief post, the sincere and delicate respect which I should always offer you, and the un-bounded confidence which on my part, if you choose, you could command, would prevent your feeling my position as anything but a form. Think of all this in a kindly spirit.'

Gladstone replied to Disraeli the same day: 'The letter you have been so kind to address to me will enable me, I trust, to remove from your mind some impressions with which you will not be sorry to part ... You consider that the relations between yourself and me have proved the main difficulty in the way of certain political arrangements. Will you allow me to assure you that I have never in my life taken a decision which turned upon them?

'You assure me that I have ever been mistaken in failing to

place you among my friends or admirers. Again, I pray you to let me say that I have never known you penurious in admiration towards anyone who had the slightest claim to it, and that at no period of my life, not even during the limited one when we were in sharp political conflict, have I either felt any enmity towards you, or believed that you felt any towards me.'

So it was that Gladstone declined this new offer. The Conservatives stayed in power until June 1859 when, once again, Palmerston, now seventy-five, became Prime Minister. He offered Gladstone any post that he cared to name. To many people's surprise Gladstone agreed to join the Government. *Gladstone declines again*

Lucy Lyttelton, Gladstone's niece, wrote in her diary on 21 June 1859: 'Uncle William has taken office under Lord Palmerston as Chancellor of the Exchequer, thereby raising an uproar in the midst of which we are shimmering, view his well-known antipathy to the Premier. What seems clear is that he considers it right to swallow personal feelings for the sake of the country ... There is this question, however: why, if he can swallow Pam, couldn't he swallow Dizzy, and, in spite of him, go in under Lord Derby? I don't pretend to be able to answer this.'

Gladstone, who remained Chancellor of the Exchequer from 1859 to 1866, became the dominant figure in public finance. His policy was to keep government expenditure as low as possible. This brought him into conflict with Palmerston, who wanted to spend more money on building up the military services. Unlike many colleagues, Gladstone did not believe that war with France was inevitable, and he worked with the Radicals to obtain a commercial treaty with the French. The Cobden Treaty was signed in 1860. While in office he swept away many customs duties —in his great budget of 1860 these were reduced from about 400 to 48—and turned Britain into a free-trade country. *Gladstone as Chancellor*

In a letter to his wife on 11 January 1860, Gladstone wrote: 'The cabinet has been again on the French treaty. There are four or five zealous, perhaps as many who would rather be without it. It has required pressure, but we have got sufficient power now, if the French will do what is reasonable. Lord John Russell has been excellent, Palmerston rather neutral.'

In a memorandum he noted the wave of anti-French feeling in

Free Trade improved relations with France, as these two cartoons suggest. *Left* Cobden teaches Louis Napoleon the principles of free trade and *right* Napoleon gives John Bull (England) the front door key, symbolic of the easing of customs barriers between the countries

the country: 'A French panic prevailed as strong as any of the other panics that have done so much discredit to this country. For this panic, the treaty of commerce with France was the only sedative. It was in fact a counter-irritant; and it aroused the sense of commercial interest to counteract the war passion. It was and is my opinion, that the choice lay between the Cobden Treaty and not the certainty, but the high probability, of a war with France.'

Disraeli thought Gladstone should not show so much disapproval of Government expenditure. He spoke in the House on 7 April 1862: 'There is something in the speeches of the Right Hon. gentleman [Gladstone] on this subject, and, indeed, on the whole of our financial system, that fills me with perplexity; which, I think, conveys to the country a sentiment, not merely of perplexity, but of distrust. And it is this, that, while the Right Hon. gentleman is without parallel or exception the most profuse Finance Minister that ever directed the affairs of this country in time of peace, he is perpetually *insinuating*—to use the mildest term—both to this

House and the country, that he disapproves of our expenditure, and that he is burning to denounce it.'

Gladstone, however, carried on just as before. In a speech at Edinburgh on 29 November 1879 he said: 'No Chancellor of the Exchequer is worth his salt who makes his own popularity either his first consideration, or any consideration at all, in administering the public purse. He is under a sacred obligation with regard to all that he consents to spend.'

When the American Civil War (1861–5) broke out, most Englishmen expected the South to win. Gladstone, though opposed to slavery, appeared to side with the rebels. During a speech at Newcastle he led his audience to believe that the Government was about to recognise the independence of the South. Disraeli was more cautious in what he said, maintaining a strict neutrality. *American Civil War*

On 29 May 1861, Gladstone wrote in a letter to the Duchess of Sutherland: 'As far as the *controversy* between North and South is a controversy on the principle announced by the Vice-President of the South, *viz.* that which asserts the superiority of the white man, and therewith founds on it his right to hold the black in slavery, I think that principle detestable, and I am wholly with the opponents of it ... No distinction can in my eyes be broader than the distinction between the question whether the Southern ideas of slavery are right, and the question whether they can justifiably be put down by war from the North.'

The following year he told the people of Newcastle-upon-Tyne: 'We may have our own opinions about slavery; we may be for or against the South; but there is no doubt that Jefferson Davis and other leaders of the South have made an army; they are making, it appears, a navy; and they have made what is more than either, they have made a nation.' (7 October 1862.)

In later years, Gladstone felt this speech had been 'an undoubted error'; 'I have yet to record ... an undoubted error ... the least excusable of them all, especially since it was committed so late in the year 1862, when I had outlived half a century. In the autumn of that year, and in a speech delivered after a public dinner at Newcastle-upon-Tyne, I declared in the heat of the American struggle that the division of the American Republic by the

During the American Civil War, a great wave of anti-slavery feeling swept England. Here is a noisy demonstration at Exeter (1863)

establishment of a Southern or secession state was an accomplished fact.

'Strange to say, this declaration, most unwarrantable to be made by a Minister of the Crown with no authority other than his own, was not due to any feeling of partisanship for the South or hostility to the North. The fortunes of the South were at their zenith ... I really, though most strangely, believed that it was an act of friendliness to all America to recognise that the struggle was virtually at an end.' (July 1896.)

In his speech on the Address in 1863, after commenting that Gladstone seemed to have given up his policy of neutrality, Disraeli said that while he himself had the greatest respect for the Southern States, he felt that England should not forget the difficulties faced by the American government.

5 Electoral Reform

BETWEEN THE PASSAGE of the Reform Act in 1832 and 1866 only two measures were passed which affected the composition of Parliament. The first abolished the property qualifications for MP's; the second removed the restrictions on Jews. Both had become law in 1858, largely due to the efforts of Disraeli himself. Now there were demands for reforms of a more sweeping nature.

The need to reform Parliament was widely accepted in Victorian England, but though many attempts had been made, since 1850, to change the franchise qualifications, all had failed for lack of agreement about the details. Following the death of Palmerston, in 1865, the Whigs (Liberals) now had a leader, Russell, who was anxious to try once more. *Reforming Parliament*

Here is an extract from Gladstone's speech on the Second Reading of the Reform Bill (12 April 1866): 'Parliament has been striving to make the working classes progressively fitter and fitter for the franchise; and can anything be more unwise, not to say more senseless, than to persevere from year to year in this plan, and then blindly to refuse to recognize its legitimate upshot—namely, the increased fitness of the working classes for the exercise of political power?' *Gladstone on reform*

The Conservatives opposed the Bill, which was narrowly defeated, and the Government resigned. Gladstone's next visit to the House of Commons was therefore as a member of the Opposition: 'Went to Windsor to take my leave. HM short but kind. H of C on return, took my place on the opposition bench, the first time for fifteen years ... Finished in Downing Street. Left my keys behind me. Somehow it makes a void.' (*Diary*, 6 July 1866.)

Russell, leader of the Whigs after Palmerston's death, sought
Parliamentary reform

*The Reform
Act, 1867*   The new Conservative Government could not ignore the problem of parliamentary reform. With Derby, the Prime Minister, in
ill-health, the responsibility for dealing with this matter fell on
Disraeli. He proposed a Bill enfranchising £6 borough householders and £20 county leaseholders, but this was later amended.
When passed, the Reform Act gave the vote in the boroughs to all
householders and £10 lodgers, and in the counties to £12 leaseholders.

Gladstone favoured a more restricted measure. Here are Disraeli's comments on his rival's behaviour, on 26 March, 1867,
during the Second Reading of the new Reform Bill: 'The Rt. Hon.
gentleman [Gladstone] gets up and addresses me in a tone which,
I must say, is very unusual in this House. Not that I at all care
for the heat he displays, although really his manner is sometimes
so very excited and so alarming that one might almost feel thank-
ful that gentlemen in this House, who sit on opposite sides of this

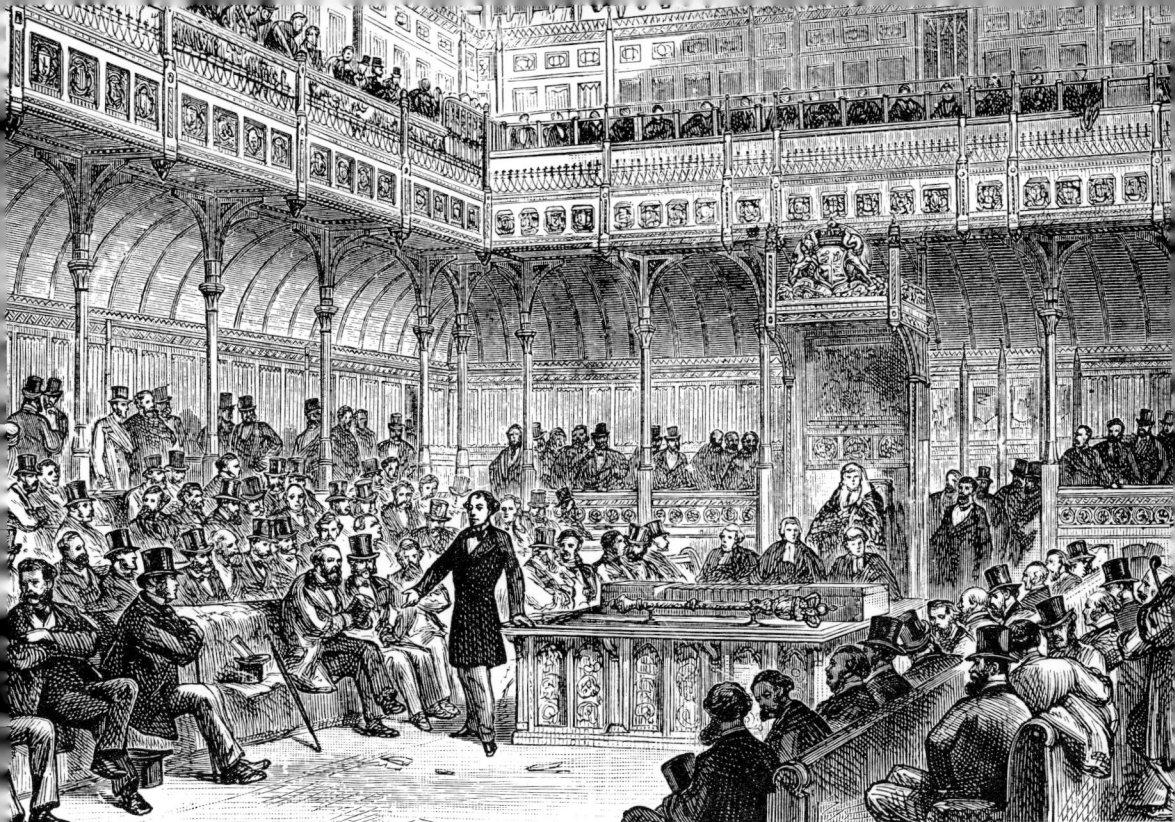

The tense scene in the Commons as Disraeli introduces his Reform Bill

table, are divided by a good broad piece of furniture!'

On 27 July 1867, *Punch* published an article on The Reform Act: *Punch's editorial (1867)* 'Unquestionably, Monday 15 July 1867, will be a Date in Anglo-Parliamentary history. For today the House of Commons passed the Reform Bill. The concluding debate, if so it may be called, was certainly unworthy of the occasion. Its main element was *Incrimination*.

'MR DISRAELI was more anxious to vindicate the measure than to defend the Government, but he addressed himself to both objects. Everybody hitherto had failed in carrying a Reform Bill. He disapproved of enfranchising a small and favoured section of the artisans, to act as a kind of Praetorian Guard ... He finished with the following blaze of glory: "I do not think myself that the country is in danger; I think England is safe in the race of men who inhabit her—that she is safe in something much more precious than her accumulated capital—her accumulated experience.

The passing of Disraeli's Reform Bill, seen through the eyes of a *Punch* cartoonist

She is safe in her national character, and her fame, in the traditions of a thousand years, and in that glorious future which I believe awaits her."

'Then the Reform Bill passed, amid cheers which proceeded chiefly from the Opposition side. On the 25 March, when the Second Reading was moved, MR GLADSTONE said, "We must make the best of the measure before us, but the prospect is very discouraging". It may be assumed that he is tolerably satisfied, but he did not take part in the concluding debate.'

Disraeli: Prime Minister The news of the Queen's acceptance of a new Prime Minister was published in *Punch* (1868): 'The Parliament which had ad-

People coming out to vote in the 1868 election

journed, in December ... reassembled on 13 February. It had been sitting only a fortnight when an important change took place in the composition of the Government—important as regards the persons concerned, but not as affecting the Ministerial Policy, which remained unchanged. LORD DERBY felt himself obliged by the state of his health, to offer his resignation as head of the Government to the Queen. This was accepted, and the Chancellor of the Exchequer (MR DISRAELI), became Prime Minister in his stead.'

But Disraeli did not remain Prime Minister for long. Gladstone urged that steps be taken to disestablish the Irish church and when the House showed sympathy with his views, Disraeli asked the Queen to dissolve Parliament. At the general election the Liberals had a majority of 112. Gladstone stood for two seats: correctly anticipating defeat in Lancashire, he also contested Greenwich, where he was successful.

Disraeli defeated

Lord Derby wrote a letter congratulating Disraeli on his

59

nomination speech: 'In the midst of our disasters, let me congratulate you, which I do very sincerely, on your speech at your nomination. It was perfectly suited to the occasion, calm, temperate, and dignified, and a striking contrast to the balderdash and braggadocio in which Gladstone has been indulging on his stumping tour.' (22 November, 1868.)

Here is a tribute to Gladstone, which *Punch* published on 12 December 1868: 'The graceful GLADSTONE has been rejected in Lancashire for a gentleman who is so large in the girth that when he had to be girt with the sword it was impossible to make the ends of the belt meet. The electors have preferred a big man to a great one.'

On 1 December 1868, Queen Victoria wrote in the third person to Gladstone requesting him to form a new government.

Gladstone: Prime Minister

Evelyn Ashley in the *National Review* (June 1868) describes the scene at Hawarden when Gladstone received the Queen's telegram: 'I was standing by him holding his coat on my arm while he in his shirt sleeves was wielding an axe to cut down a tree. Up came a telegraph messenger. He took the telegram, opened it and read it, then handed it to me, speaking only two words, "Very significant", and at once resumed his work. The message merely stated that General Grey would arrive that evening from Windsor. This of course implied that a mandate was coming from the Queen charging Mr Gladstone with the formation of his first government …

'After a few minutes the blows ceased, and Mr Gladstone resting on the handle of his axe, looked up and with deep earnestness in his voice and with great intensity in his face, exclaimed, "My mission is to pacify Ireland." He then resumed his task, and never said another word till the tree was down.'

Punch published this rhyme on 19 December 1868:

> *Gone is* DIZZY;
> *From the busy*
> *Cares of State repose he can.*
> *In comes* GLADDY,
> *Who of* PADDY
> *Means to make a loyal man.*

Opposite The many faces of Disraeli, drawn by Tenniel and others. His prominent nose and flamboyant manner provided a splendid butt for the cartoonists

6 Gladstone and the Irish

WHEN THE BRITISH AND IRISH Parliaments were united on 1 January 1801, it was hoped that this would provide a solution to the troubles which had divided the two countries for so long. In fact, the Act of Union did nothing to quench the demands of the Irish for more freedom, and by the 1860s there was a growing movement for Home Rule—complete independence.

Throughout the nineteenth century the Irish fretted at British *Irish troubles* rule. They resented the dominance of the Church of England in a mainly Catholic country. They resented the widespread poverty, and the political control exercised by Westminster. The struggle for greater independence was fought both by the group of Irish MP's in the Commons and by revolutionary movements in Ireland itself. In 1858, Irish immigrants in the United States formed the Fenian Society.

In *Four Years of Irish History: 1845–1849* (1883) C. G. Duffy wrote: 'The condition of Ireland at the opening of the year 1847 is one of the most painful chapters in the annals of mankind. An industrious and hospitable race was now in the pangs of a devouring famine. Deaths of individuals, of husband and wife, of entire families were becoming common. The potato-blight had spread from the Atlantic to the Caspian, but there was more suffering in the parish of Mayo than in all the rest of Europe. From Connaught, where distress was greatest, there came batches of inquests, with the horrible verdict "died of starvation". In some cases the victims were buried "wrapped in a coarse coverlet", a coffin being too costly a luxury. The living awaited death with a listlessness which was at once tragic and revolting. Women with

63

Opposite Gladstone explains to the Commons his scheme for the Government of Ireland, 1886

In the 1841 Irish famine, starving mobs attacked grain ships

dead children in their arms, were seen begging for a coffin to bury them in.'

The Fenians   The violence that the Society used was described in *The Illustrated Times* (16 February 1867): 'The Fenians have recently organised in New York a band of fifty, whose special mission it is to proceed to England and Ireland and endeavour to resuscitate the dying brotherhood. These men are understood to have arrived in England ... A meeting was called for Sunday at Liverpool and it was then resolved to attack Chester Castle the following day, seize the arms deposited there, cut the telegraph wires, tear up the rails, and make good their escape by rail to Holyhead and trust to fortune to get across to Ireland ... The first intimation received in Chester of the intended raid was at 12.30 am by Mr Fenwick from Superintendent Ryde of Liverpool and was to the effect that an ex-officer of the American Army, who produced his commission

A secret Fenian dynamite factory discovered in Birmingham

as an officer of the Fenian service, had revealed the whole plot to them. Prompt measures were taken and the commandant telegraphed to Manchester for reinforcements.

'Mr Fenwick next went to the station and gave instructions for the trains to be watched as they arrived. At 2.30 a batch of thirty fellows arrived from Liverpool, and were evidently under the control of an officer. They were soon followed by further detachments from thirty to sixty from Liverpool, and some from Manchester, all of similar experience. They dispersed quietly into the town. Early in the morning the volunteers were called out. They were sworn in as special constables ... it was ascertained that the Fenians numbered 1,400 to 1,500. A number of men who were supposed to be their leaders collected at a house where the police had been informed they would meet for orders ...

'At night the Mayor called a public meeting ... and over 500

D

citizens were sworn in as special constables ... the Fenians evidently came to the conclusion that the preparations were too much for them, and as the night advanced, parties of tens and twenties were seen leaving, on foot, for Warrington and other neighbouring towns.'

Gladstone anxiously watched these events. How could rebellion in Ireland be prevented? Shortly after taking office he introduced a Bill into Parliament to 'disestablish and disendow the Protestant Church in Ireland'. The Conservatives and many of the English clergy were against the measure, and though it passed easily through the Commons, it had a more difficult passage in the House of Lords where the bishops sat.

Punch reported in 1869: 'The main business of the Session commenced on the 1 March, when MR GLADSTONE moved the first reading of the Bill in a speech of three hours' duration ... The Second Reading of the Bill, which was resolutely opposed by MR DISRAELI and the Conservative party, gave rise to a long and remarkable debate, lasting for several nights, and terminating in a division, which gave the Government the decisive majority of 118 in a House of as many as 618 Members. The Committee on the Bill was taken after the Easter Recess, and "although a few alterations of minor importance were conceded, the efforts of the Opposition to expunge and alter any of the principal features of the Bill were quite unavailing". ... after many debates and divisions the Third Reading was carried on the last day of May by a majority of 114, the numbers being 361 to 247 ...

'The Bill was introduced into the House of Lords after the Whitsuntide recess. EARL GRANVILLE, as the Ministerial Leader in the Upper House, moved the Second Reading on the 14 June, and was followed by the EARL OF HARROWBY, who proposed its rejection. A very remarkable debate followed. In the course of it, the late EARL OF DERBY made the last great speech he was ever to deliver in Parliament. The deceased Bishop of St David's (THIRLWALL), supported the measure, and the Bishop of Peterborough (MAGEE), opposed it—both these eminent Prelates displaying consummate power and ability in their addresses. The Second Reading was carried by a majority of thirty-three, the BISHOP OF ST DAVID'S being the only Member of the Episcopal Bench who

67

Opposite Gladstone was determined to pacify Ireland. Tenniel's cartoon suggests that, with the passing of the Irish Land Act, he saw himself as the country's saviour

Eviction of a poor Irish family (1870), a tragic and common scene

voted with the Government in favour of the Bill. In Committee important amendments were carried by the Opposition ...

' "The most remarkable legislative achievement of modern times" was completed by the Bill receiving the Royal assent and passing into law on the 26 July.'

Disraeli was far-sighted in what he had to say: 'What I fear in the policy of the Right Hon. gentleman [Gladstone] is that its tendency is to civil war. I am not surprised that Hon. gentlemen should for a moment be startled by such an expression. Let them think a little. Is it natural and probable that the Papal power in Ireland will attempt to attain ascendency and predominance? I say it is natural. And what is more, it ought to do it.

'Is it natural that the Protestants of Ireland should submit without a struggle to such a state of things? You know they will not; that is settled. Is England to interfere? Are we again to conquer Ireland? Are we to have a repetition of the direful history which on both sides now we wish to forget? Is there to be another Battle of the Boyne, another Siege of Derry, another Treaty of Limerick? These things are not only possible, but probable. You are commencing a policy which will inevitably lead to such results.' (Speech in the Commons on the Third Reading of the Irish Church Bill, 31 May 1869.)

Gladstone first turned his attention to the land question. Nearly all land in Ireland was owned by Englishmen, from whom the Irish had to rent it at high prices. The object of the Irish Land Act (1870) was to prevent landlords turning out their tenants without giving them compensation for eviction. This, however, only solved part of the problem and did little to end the unrest in the country. The Government was forced to introduce a Coercion Act in an effort to preserve peace. *Preserving the peace*

The Government was accused of apathy towards the Irish problem. On 2 April 1870, *Punch* recorded: 'Some people blame the Government for its apparent apathy respecting the foul outrages and murders rife in Ireland. The Government may answer that force has proved a failure; that theirs is a pacific and not repressive policy; that their Church Bill and their Land Bill will satisfy all claims for justice at our hands; and that these sedatives are certain, in course of time, to cure. The Government may, doubtless, have fair grounds for their opinion, but there are some good judges who differ from such judgment. Among them may be cited LORD CHIEF JUSTICE WHITESIDE, who, referring to the threatenings, and pistollings, and riotings so terribly rife now, is reported to have said: "If this awful state of things be allowed to continue, if crime goes thus undetected, the result will be that the people will consider themselves safer under the protection of these skulking murderers than under that of the law. If crime goes unpunished, then the result must be that the arm of the law will be paralysed, and its administration impossible." '

On 26 March, *Punch* satirized Gladstone's efforts to solve the growing Irish problem:

As I was walkun St Stephen's hard by, *Gladstone*
I heerd a gurt hullaballoo in a sty, *satirized*
Where grunt, squake, and snort in rough music did jine,
And there was BILL GLADSTONE a feedun his swine.

They run and reared up, they gnashed tusks, pushed wi' snout;
I thinks they'd ha gored un could they ha got out.
I never afore zee sich tumult and strife,
Goo on in a pigsty the whole o' my life.

I says to'n, I says, 'Bill, why, what pigs be they,
That thanks for their vittles returns that queer way?'
'Them there precious pigs,' says BILL GLADSTONE, says he,
'Them riotous hogs, they be Irish, they be.'

Says I, 'What pervuss pigs in Ireland is bred!
Wun't aven bide quiet the whilst they are fed.'
'I'm sorry,' says WILLUM, 'to say, no, they wun't,
The more they gits given 'um the wuss they do grunt.

'In this place afore me chaps long ha' took pains
To plase 'um wi' wash and to coax 'um wi' grains.
Now, I've ben a tryun to zilunce their squeal
Wi' Liberal mizures o' best barley-meal.'

'Their troughs thee mayst cause to run over wi' swill;'
I says; 'barley-meal thee mayst gorge 'um wi', Bill;
Pearl-barley them pigs thee mayst offer at last;
Thee't find that thy pearls afore swine thee't ha' cast.

' 'Tis time them unruly pigs now for to check
Wi' rings droo the nose and a clog round the neck.
If that means doan't answer, then curry their hides;
Drap into they hogs wi' a broomstick besides.

'As justus and kindness thee fully hast tried,
They's now got the 'vantidge o' right on thy side:
Zo put forth thy might for to back thy right by,
And Peace Preservation enfoorce in the sty.'

70

7 Liberalism in Action

GLADSTONE WAS COMMITTED to a policy of social justice and national efficiency. The Government introduced a programme of reforms, far exceeding anything that Parliament had seen since the time of Peel. It dealt with a wide range of subjects, some of which we will now examine.

What was the Liberal view of education?

Educating 'our masters'

Before 1870 all plans to establish a national system of elementary education had come to nothing because of the sharp religious differences which divided the nation. Since 1833, governments had been content to pay grants to a number of voluntary bodies—the National Society (Anglican) and the British and Foreign Society (Nonconformist) were the largest of these—which maintained their own schools. But this system could not provide enough school places to meet the growing need—a need which Robert Lowe believed had been made greater by the Reform Act.

In a speech in the Commons on the Third Reading of the Reform Bill, Lowe explained: 'I suppose now it will be absolutely necessary to educate our masters. I was before this opposed to centralization [in education]; I am now ready to accept centralization. I was opposed to an education rate; I am now ready to accept one ... The question is no longer a religious question; it has become a political one ... You have placed the government in the hands of the masses, and you must therefore give them education.'

An Education Bill was piloted through the House of Commons by W. E. Forster, who was Vice-President of the Education Department. 'Last year I moved the Education Estimate, and in addition to the money required for the central office, for Inspec-

71

tors and for normal schools (training colleges for teachers), I asked for an annual grant of about £415,000 for primary schools in England and Wales. Of those schools about 11,000 were day schools and 2,000 night schools. The number of children upon the registers of those schools was about 1,450,000, and the average

W. E. Forster, the man chiefly responsible for the 1870 Education Act

attendance about 1,000,000, representing, therefore, the education more or less imperfect of nearly 1,500,000 children ...

'But as I had the honour of stating last year, only two-fifths of the children of the working-classes between the ages of six and ten years are on the registers of the Government schools, and only one-third of those between the ages of ten and twelve. Consequently, of those between six and ten, we have helped about 700,000, more or less, but we have left unhelped 1,000,000; while of those between ten and twelve, we have helped 250,000, and left unhelped at least 500,000 ...'

Forster continued: 'It is calculated that in Liverpool the number of children between five and thirteen who ought to receive an elementary education is 80,000. But as far as we can ascertain, 20,000 of them attend no school whatever, while at least another 20,000 attend schools where they get an education not worth having. In Manchester—not including Salford—there are about 65,000 children who might be at school, and of this number about 16,000 go to no school at all ... As a Yorkshireman, I am sorry to say that, from what I hear, Leeds appears to be as bad as Liverpool; and so also, I fear, is Birmingham ...

'To its honour, Parliament has lately decided that England shall in future be governed by popular government. I am one of those who would not wait until the people were educated before I would trust them with political power. If we had thus waited, we might have waited long for education; but now that we have given them political power we must not wait any longer to give them education.' (17 February 1870.)

The Education Act stated: 'There shall be provided for every *Education* public school district a sufficient amount of accommodation in *Act (1870)* public elementary schools (as hereinafter defined) available for all the children resident in such district for whose elementary education efficient and suitable provision is not otherwise made; and where there is an insufficient amount of such accommodation, in this Act referred to as "public school accommodation", the deficiency shall be supplied in the manner provided by this Act.'

This Act is thought by many to be the greatest achievement of Gladstone's first Ministry, but the Prime Minister played little part in framing it. He wrote to Lord Granville on 14 June 1874: 'I have never made greater personal concessions of opinion than I did on the Education bill to the united representations of Ripon and Forster.'

The Conservatives welcomed the extension of elementary schooling and, under Disraeli's direction, gave the Act their support.

The Education Act was but one of many measures in the great *Army reforms* programme of Liberal reforms. In 1871 the Government set about 73 reforming the army. Edward Cardwell, the War Secretary, began by abolishing flogging as a peacetime military punishment. Then he brought in an Army Regulation Bill, 'the object of which was to combine in one harmonious whole all the branches of our military forces'. The Bill met with stiff opposition, particularly from army Members ('the Colonels') who disliked the provision to stop the practice of purchasing commissions. At last it passed through the Commons, only to face defeat in the Lords. Gladstone angered MPs, including Disraeli who approved of the reforms, when he now advised the Queen to abolish 'purchase' by Royal Warrant. Disraeli called it a 'shameful and avowed conspiracy of the cabinet against the privileges' of the House of Lords.

A. E. Freeman, however, writing in the *Pall Mall Gazette* on 12 February 1874 tried to explain Gladstone's actions: 'I believe that this is one of those cases in which a strictly conscientious man like Mr Gladstone does things from which a less conscientious man would shrink. Such a man, fully convinced of his own integrity, often thinks less than it would be wise to think of mere appearances, and so lays himself open to the imputation of motives poles asunder from the real ones.'

Trade unions The legal position of trade unions was confused, and the Liberals were anxious about this. The right to strike, the right to persuade workers not to blackleg during a strike and the right for a union to be recognised as a corporation were all in dispute. The Conservative Government had set up a Royal Commission in 1867 to look into such matters and between then and 1869 it produced eleven reports.

On the basis of its findings, the Liberals worked out a Trade Union Bill which became law in 1871. This for the first time enabled unions to own property, and to take action in a court of law. But, to the dismay of trade unionists, Parliament also passed a Criminal Law Amendment Act which prohibited picketing, even when peaceful.

Here is the eleventh and final report from the Conservative Trades Union Commission (1869): 'It is common to take for granted that the objects of unionism are to raise the wages and to shorten the hours of labour, the means to this end being the threat of or resort to a strike. It is supposed to follow from this that whatever tends to increase the machinery and power of a union tends to increase the frequency and magnitude of strikes.

'This is a proposition ... that is far from being borne out by the evidence before us. Little would be gained by attempting to give any precise formula for the objects aimed at by unionism, where the nature and spirit of the actual unions differ so widely. But the most general description which appears to us to correspond with the facts is this: that unions are associations of workmen for mutual assistance in securing generally the most favourable conditions of labour ...

'It may very well be allowed that if not the principal, at any rate one of the most constant, objects of the unions is to obtain for the workmen the best rate of wages which their services will command, and then to reduce the number of hours in which the wages are to be earned ...

'Under a system which professes the right or rather the duty of all men peacefully to pursue their own interests for themselves, unionism appears to us the exact correlative to competition. The stronger prefer to pursue their ends by means of competition, the weaker by means of combination. But for the capitalist to deny the workman unlimited freedom to combine, is for the stronger to object to the weaker pursuing his interests by the most obvious resource in his reach ... THOMAS HUGHES, FREDERICK HARRISON.'

G. Howell wrote in *Labour Legislation, Labour Movements and Labour Leaders* (1902): 'The agitation evoked by the Criminal Law Amendment Act ... was widespread, systematic and thorough. It was an organised demand for the repeal of a bad law, intentionally levelled at workmen, especially when acting collectively ... The Trade Union Act gave to men in combinations rights too long withheld, but in giving those rights the legislature insulted the recipients, and provided a weapon for their castigation ...'

The old subject of electoral reform was another current topic. *Secret ballot* Ever since the first Reform Act in 1832 opinions in the country had been divided about the secret ballot. The Chartists had made it one of their Six Points. Many politicians, however, including Gladstone, believed that open voting was more democratic.

But as a result of the second Reform Act, more working men had the vote. Secrecy at elections seemed the only sure way of

Overleaf February 1867: the great Trade Union demonstration in Waterloo Place, London

protecting them from irate employers who might disagree with the way they voted. The Liberals brought in a Ballot Bill in 1871, but it was defeated in the Lords. In 1872, the Bill was again passed through the Commons and this time the Upper House gave way. Disraeli proposed a plan for optional secrecy and hoped that the Lords could force this as an amendment.

In a speech at Greenwich on 21 December, 1868 Gladstone said: 'I have at all times given my vote in favour of open voting, but I have done so before, and I do so now, with an important reservation, namely, that whether by open voting or by whatsoever means, free voting must be secured.'

On 20 July 1872, *Punch* reported: 'After a dignified discussion (in the course of which EARL RUSSELL mentioned, from his personal knowledge, that MR GLADSTONE had "over and over" voted against the Ballot), the Peers gave up the Optional Secrecy Clause by 157 to 138, majority nineteen, and they also gave up their objection to using schools for voting places, a concession for which the children who will get holidays on polldays, ought not to be grateful, but will be.'

The Ballot Act 1872 — Here are the main points of the Ballot Act (1872): 'In the case of a poll at an election the votes shall be given by ballot. The ballot of each voter shall consist of a paper (in this Act called a ballot paper) showing the names and descriptions of the candidates. Each ballot paper shall have a number printed on the back, and shall have attached a counterfoil with the same number printed on the face.

'At the time of voting, the ballot paper shall be marked on both sides with an official mark, and delivered to the voter within the polling station, and the number of such voter on the register of voters shall be marked on the counterfoil, and the voter having secretly marked his vote on the paper, and folded it up so as to conceal his vote, shall place it in a closed box in the presence of the officer presiding at the polling station (in this Act called "the presiding officer") after having shown to him the official mark at the back.'

8 Losing Support

ANY GOVERNMENT WHICH EMBARKS upon an extensive programme of reforms must expect to run into difficulties. Every measure proposed is likely to upset some vested interest. Gladstone's ministry certainly aroused plenty of opposition. A Licensing Act (1872), for example, designed to remedy some of the evils in the sale of drink, not only angered the liquor trade, but was resented by many workmen. Whatever the legislation, there were people ready to object. Gladstone and the Liberals slowly began to lose the popularity which had swept them into power in 1868.

The country expected financial wonders from Gladstone's *Cabinet of* Government. His cabinet contained five men who were at one *financiers* time or another Chancellors of the Exchequer, though it was Robert Lowe who currently held the office. Gladstone was still committed to keeping down public expenditure. He wrote to Lowe listing some measures which he had tried to introduce without success and suggesting other possible reforms:

'I have referred to my list of remnants; and I will begin with those that I tried in Parliament and failed in: (1) collection of taxes by Queen's officers instead of local officers, (2) taxation of charities, (3) Bill for restraining, with a view to ultimately abolishing, the circulation of the notes of private banks, (4) plan for bringing the Chancery and other judicial accounts under the control of parliament ...

'The following are subjects which I was not able to take in hand: (1) abolition of the remaining duty upon corn, an exceeding strong case, (2) I should be much disposed to abolish the tea licenses as greatly restrictive of the consumption of a dutiable and useful commodity. I modified them; but am not sure that this was enough ... (3) The probate duty calls, I fear, loudly for change; but I wanted either time or courage to take it in hand. (4) The remaining conveyance duties, apart from railways, I always considered as marked for extinction ... (5) The fire insurance duty is sure to be further assailed. Though not as bad (relatively to other taxes) as is supposed, it is bad enough to be very hard to defend in an adverse House ... (6) The income tax at 6*d*, I suppose, presents a forward claim. (7) The commutation of malt duty for beer duty must always, I presume, be spoken of with respect; but the working objections to it have thus far been found too hard to deal with.

'There is always room in detail for amendments of stamp duties ...

'This is all I need trouble you with, and I have endeavoured to keep clear of all idiosyncratic propositions as much as in me lies. Of course such a letter calls for no answer. As this legacy opinion to you takes the form of a donation *inter vivos* it will, I hope, escape duty.' (9 January 1869.)

Morley wrote: 'When Mr Gladstone was at the exchequer the charge on naval, military, and civil expenditure had been reduced between 1860 and 1865 from £38 m to £31 m. Under the Derby-Disraeli government the figure rose in two or three years to £34¾ m. By 1873 it had been brought down again to little more than £32¼ m.'

'Harum-scarum' budget

Disraeli scornfully called Lowe's budgets 'harum-scarum'. They ran into trouble in the House and helped to make the Liberals unpopular with many of the electorate. The budget of 1871 was especially ill-received. The need to find money for the proposed army reforms meant that taxation had to be increased.

'*Thursday* was the night of the Great Event. The House was crammed ... MR GLADSTONE delivered a somewhat long speech on the Budget. This it had been necessary to reconsider as a whole. The Government stood by their Estimates, would not tax articles of great consumption, would not borrow money. But the proposals as to the Succession Duties would be abandoned, and so would the proposal to change the mode of levying the Income-tax from poundage to percentage.

'But how is the money to be obtained?

A cartoon showing Disraeli roasting his unpopular Liberal opponents,
after he had criticised their policies in 1873

'Need you ask?

'The Income-tax?

'Of course. What else? The extra Twopence is to be laid on, and
henceforth the real Working Men are to pay Sixpence in the
Pound.

'We bear it, and therefore we deserve to bear it. Let us do so,
and grin with what contortions we may.

'The debate was very amusing. MR DISRAELI, of course, had no
need to make his hostile motion, but he remarked that this year
direct taxation had been increased by three millions. The Budget
he described as now one of "sweet simplicity".'

War, too, had been a major topic of discussion. Gladstone
wrote to Michael Chevalier a few days after the start of the
Franco-Prussian war in July 1870. 'I cannot describe to you the
sensation of pain, almost of horror, which has thrilled through
this country from end to end at the outbreak of hostilities ... I
suppose there was a time when England would have said, "Let
our neighbours, being as they are, our rivals, waste their energies,

81

The rout of the French troops at the Battle of Sedan

their wealth, their precious irrevocable lives, in destroying one another: they will be the weaker, we shall be relatively the stronger.'' But we have now unlearned that bad philosophy; and the war between France and Prussia saddens the whole face of society, and burdens every man with a personal grief.'

Disraeli's 'armed neutrality'

There was little that Britain could do about the war except follow a policy of neutrality. Disraeli agreed but, in a speech on 1 August, he declared that it must be an armed neutrality. Were our military resources strong enough, he asked, to enable us to pursue such a policy? *Punch* reported: Monday, August 1. The House of Commons was crowded, MR DISRAELI having given notice that he should speak on foreign affairs. The leader of the Opposition declared that in war-times great injury had been done by too much silence and reserve on the part of the British Parliament. He therefore intended to try to induce Government to speak out ... In what

Napoleon III and the Empress Eugenie lived in lonely exile in England after the Franco-Prussian War, 1870

condition were our Army, Navy, Militia, and Volunteers? Had we been reducing expenses too much for safety?'

Disraeli's views on the war are expressed in a letter to Lord Derby, written on 17 August 1870: 'I do not much believe in the great battle, which they say is going on. The French are in full retreat on their whole line, and the Prussians, as is usual under such circumstances, are following them up and harassing them. Being strong in cavalry, the Germans have an additional advantage.

'This collapse of France has all come from the Emperor's policy of nationality. That has created Italy and Germany, which has destroyed the French monopoly of Continental compactness. The Emperor started this hare in order that he might ultimately get Belgium. Belgium is safe and France is smashed! ...

'England is busy at mediation, but Prussia thinks the Gauls are not yet sufficiently humiliated. Russia jealous of Prussia, yet hating France—England strong in words, but a mediation of phrases won't do.'

He wrote again on 27 November 1870: 'The Government appear to be in trouble, and probably will continue to be so. Whatever their ultimate decision, these matters take time. But, no doubt, however they may act, their embarrassment must be great, for they can hardly avoid proposing increased armaments.'

Disraeli addressed the House of Commons on the 9 February 1871: 'Let me impress upon the attention of the House the character of this war between France and Germany. It is no common war, like the war between Prussia and Austria, or like the Italian war in which France was engaged some years ago; nor is it like the Crimean War. This war represents the German revolution, a greater political event than the French revolution of last century. I don't say a greater, or as great a social event. What its social consequences may be are in the future. Not a single principle in the management of our foreign affairs, accepted by all statesmen for guidance up to six months ago, any longer exists. There is not a diplomatic tradition which has not been swept away.

'You have a new world, new influences at work, new and unknown objects and dangers with which to cope, at present involved in that obscurity incident to novelty in such affairs. We used to have discussions in this House about the balance of power. Lord Palmerston, eminently a practical man, trimmed the ship of State and shaped its policy with a view to preserve an equilibrium in Europe ...

'But,' he asked, 'what has really come to pass? The balance of power has been entirely destroyed, and the country which suffers most, and feels the effects of this great change most, is England.'

The war ended in February 1871, with the French being forced to cede the provinces of Alsace and Lorraine to the Germans.

Disraeli in opposition
By early 1872 it was apparent that Gladstone and the Liberals had lost their wide support in the country. At the same time Disraeli enjoyed a popularity such as he had never known before.

Sir William Fraser recalled: 'On returning from St Paul's, Disraeli met with an overpowering "ovation"; I should say "triumph", for he was in his chariot ... the cheers which greeted him from all classes convinced him that, for the day at least, a more popular man did not exist in England.'

Disraeli now attacked the Government with renewed ferocity. In a speech in Manchester given on 3 April 1872 he declared: 'Extravagance is being substituted for energy by the Government. The unnatural stimulus is subsiding. Their paroxysms end in prostration.

'Some take refuge in melancholy, and their eminent chief alternates between menace and a sigh. As I sit opposite the Treasury Bench, the ministers remind me of one of those marine landscapes not very unusual on the coasts of South America. You behold a range of exhausted volcanoes! Not a flame flickers upon a single pallid crest! But the situation is still dangerous. There are occasional earthquakes, and ever and anon the dark rumblings of the sea.'

And in the House of Commons on 11 March 1873: 'You [Gladstone's Government] have had four years of it. You have despoiled churches. You have threatened every corporation and endowment in the country. You have criticised every profession and vexed every trade. No one is certain of his property and nobody knows what duties he may have to perform tomorrow.'

In March 1873 the Government was at last defeated in the *Gladstone* Commons and Gladstone resigned. Disraeli was invited by the *resigns* Queen to form a Ministry, but he declined. He and the Conservatives wanted nothing less than a general election, hoping for a landslide victory. Gladstone then agreed to resume office, and so parliamentary business continued.

On 21 March 1873, after this incident, Gladstone wrote to his brother, Robertson, that despite their differences, both political and personal: 'I sometimes think he and I might with advantage pair off together.'

9 On Top of the Greasy Pole

THE LIBERAL GOVERNMENT came to the end of its course in 1874. After the election it was replaced by a Ministry with Disraeli as Prime Minister. For a time, opposition to the Conservatives was weak and divided, with the Radicals and the Irish creating the greatest difficulties. Gladstone, in fact, went into semi-retirement in 1875. Victoria was delighted with the change of government and Disraeli enjoyed the confidence of the Crown as no Prime Minister had done since the days of Melbourne.

The end of 1873 had been an unhappy time for Gladstone's Government, and the Liberals had suffered a number of by-election defeats. In the general election, Disraeli's Conservatives won a majority of about sixty in the new House, the first workable majority that they had had since the days of Peel.

Real power at last

Queen Victoria wrote in a memorandum of 18 February 1874: 'Mr Disraeli came at half past twelve. He expressed great surprise at the result of the elections. He had thought there might have been a very small majority for them; but nothing like this had been anticipated, and no party organization could have caused this result of a majority of nearly sixty-four. Not since the time of Pitt and Fox had there been anything like it. Even in 1841 when such a large majority had been returned for Sir R. Peel, it had not been so extraordinary, because he had had a small majority. It justified, he said, the course he had pursued last March in declining to take office ... He was anxious to bring as much new talent and blood into the Government as possible.'

Once before, in 1868, Disraeli had held the premiership for a few months. On that occasion he told his friends, 'I have climbed

87

Opposite Disraeli at last achieved the Premiership on the resignation of Lord Derby to the top of the greasy pole.' He was to occupy that position for the next six years.

Gladstone takes a back seat The long period in office had exhausted Gladstone, who, at sixty-five, was a tired man. As soon as defeat seemed likely he decided to resign as leader of the Liberal party, though another year was to pass before he actually took this step. Although continuing as an MP, he was now often absent from the House and spent much of his time studying theology, a subject which had long interested him.

In a letter to his brother, Robertson, he wrote: 'I do not intend to assume the general functions of leader of the Opposition, and my great ambition or design will be to spend the remainder of my days, if it please God, in tranquillity, and at any rate in freedom from political strife.' (6 February 1874.)

He sought 'an interval between Parliament and the grave.' 'I was most anxious to make the retirement of the ministry the occasion of my own. I had served for more than forty years. My age, sixty-five, was greater than that of Sir Robert Peel at his retirement in 1846, or at his death in 1850, and was much beyond that at which most of the leading commoners of the century had terminated their political career, together with their natural life.'

Gladstone's religion Early in April 1874, he wrote to his wife: 'The anti-parliamentary reaction has been stronger with me than I anticipated. I am as far as possible from feeling the want of the House of Commons. I could cheerfully go there to do a work; but I hope and pray to be as little there as possible, except for such an aim ...

'There is one thing I should like you to understand clearly as to my view of things, for it is an essential part of that view. I am convinced that the welfare of mankind does not now depend on the state or the world of politics; the real battle is being fought in the world of thought, where a deadly attack is made with great tenacity of purpose and over a wide field, upon the greatest treasure of mankind, the belief in God and the gospel of Christ.'

The Queen's favourite Disraeli began his Ministry confident that he had the support of the Queen. Victoria had grown suspicious of Liberalism, which she saw as a threat to the prestige of the Crown. As for Gladstone, her feelings towards him fluctuated between disapproval and contempt.

Queen Victoria wrote in a letter to the Crown Princess of Prussia on 24 February 1874: 'Lord Palmerston was quite right when he said to me "Mr Gladstone is a very dangerous man". And so very arrogant, tyrannical and obstinate with no knowledge of the World or human nature. Papa felt this strongly. Then he was a fanatic in religion—All this and much want of regard towards my feelings (though since I was so ill that was better) led to make him a very dangerous and unsatisfactory Premier. He was a bad Leader of the House of Commons.'

A good relationship between the Queen and the Conservative leader had been established over many years. On the death of Prince Albert, for example, Victoria had sent Disraeli a bound copy of her husband's speeches. Here is her covering letter, written on 24 April 1863: 'The Queen cannot resist from expressing personally, to Mr Disraeli her deep gratification at the tribute he paid her adored, beloved, and great husband. The perusal of it made her shed many tears, but it was very soothing to her broken heart to see such true appreciation of that spotless and unequalled character.

'The Queen asks Mr Disraeli to accept the accompanying book.'

In 1868, after Disraeli's first period as Prime Minister, Victoria agreed to his request to confer a peerage on his wife: 'The Queen has received Mr Disraeli's letter, and has much pleasure in complying with his request that she should confer a peerage on Mrs Disraeli, as a mark of her sense of his service. The Queen thinks that Mr Disraeli, with whom she will part with much regret, can render her most useful service even when not in office ...

Lady Beaconsfield

'The Queen can indeed truly sympathise with his devotion to Mrs Disraeli, who in her turn is so deeply attached to him, and she hopes they may yet enjoy many years of happiness together.

'The Queen will gladly confer the title of Viscountess Beaconsfield on Mrs Disraeli.' (Letter dated 24 November 1868.)

Disraeli continued to be the Queen's favourite minister. After he returned from the Congress of Berlin she wrote to him: 'The Queen thanks Lord Beaconsfield very much for his very kind letter of the 13th, and sends these lines with some Windsor flowers to welcome him back in triumph! ...

Hero of Berlin (1878)

'The Queen is much grieved to hear ... that he has been so

89

suffering from his old enemy [gout], but she trusts that by this time he is already much better. The exertions he has made have been so great that the Queen has always been living in fear of some such attack. But he has achieved so much that that will help to make him well.

'He *must now* accept the Garter. She must insist on it.

'It will be a disappointment not to see Lord Beaconsfield so soon, but he must be very careful and husband his strength for Parliament. The Convention and possession of Cyprus has given immense satisfaction to the country. High and low are delighted, excepting Mr Gladstone, who is frantic.' (Letter dated 16 July 1878.)

'To put down ritualism'

Disraeli was in ill-health for much of the time that he was Prime Minister. As well as gout, he also suffered from asthma and kidney disease. Although a strong and able premier, old age and illness had taken their toll of this dynamic personality. He admitted that power had come to him too late.

Viscount Cross wrote in his *A Political History* (1903): 'From all his speeches I had quite expected that [Disraeli's] mind was full of legislative schemes, but such did not prove to be the case; on the contrary he had to entirely rely on suggestions of his colleagues, and as they themselves had only just come into office, and that suddenly, there was some difficulty in framing the Queen's speech.'

Disraeli's Government was soon caught up in an ecclesiastical storm. The Archbishop of Canterbury introduced a Private Member's Bill designed to put down 'ritualism' in the Protestant Church. (Ritualism involved such practices as the wearing of vestments when celebrating the sacraments, the mixing of water and wine in the sacramental cup and the use of incense and altar lights.) The Queen urged Disraeli to support the Bill. His decision to do so brought him, once again, into conflict with Gladstone who made a fierce, but unsuccessful, attempt to amend it.

In a letter to Disraeli, written on 10 July 1874, the Queen once again expressed her regret at Gladstone's conduct: 'She [the Queen] is deeply grieved to see the want of Protestant feeling in the Cabinet. Mr Gladstone's conduct is much to be regretted, though it is not surprising: but she wrote to him in the strongest terms of the danger to the Church and of the intention of the Archbishop

By treating Victoria (*left*) as a woman first and a Queen second, Disraeli
(*right*) was always her favourite

to bring forward a measure to try and regulate the shameful
practices of the Ritualists.

'He [Disraeli] should state to the Cabinet how strongly the
Queen feels and how faithful she is to the Protestant faith, to
defend and maintain which, her family was placed upon the
Throne! She owns she often asks herself what has become of the
Protestant feeling of Englishmen.'

On receipt of Disraeli's reply, she wrote again next day to him
offering her thanks: 'The Queen thanks Mr Disraeli for his letter
which is very reassuring. It is a *most* important question. Mr
Disraeli must have managed his refractory Cabinet most skilfully.'

About this time, Gladstone wrote a magazine article on *Disraeli on*
Ritualism. Here is Disraeli's opinion of it in a letter to Lady *ritualism*
Bradford on 5 October 1874: 'I have read Gladstone, but with
difficulty. He is a cumbrous writer. Now for the substance, how-

ever: nothing. He does not meet the great question, which every instant is becoming greater.

'All—at least all civilised beings—must be for the "beauty of holiness". No one stronger than myself. In ecclesiastical affairs I require order, taste, ceremony. But these are quite compatible with a sincere profession of the established religion of the country. What I object to is the introduction of a peculiar set of ceremonies, which are avowedly symbolical of doctrines which that Established Church was instituted, and is supported, to refute and to repudiate. This is what the people of England are thinking of. His article is mere "leather and prunella".'

10 For Queen and Empire

AS A 'YOUNG ENGLANDER', many years before, Disraeli had upheld the need to strengthen the Monarchy. In June 1872 he returned to this theme, and outlined a new policy for the Conservative party in which the Crown would be the focal point in the British Empire. Now in office, he arranged for the Queen to be created Empress of India.

Disraeli had become increasingly absorbed with foreign and imperial affairs. On 3 April 1872, he addressed a meeting in Manchester: 'The very phrase "foreign affairs" makes an Englishman convinced that I am about to treat of subjects with which he has no concern. Unhappily the relations of England with the rest of the world, which are "foreign affairs", are the matters which most influence his lot. Upon them depends the increase or reduction of taxation. Upon them depends the enjoyment or the embarrassment of his industry. And yet, though so momentous are the consequences of the mismanagement of our foreign relations, no one thinks of them till the mischief occurs, and then it is found how the most vital consequences have been occasioned by mere inadvertence ...'

The rest of the world

But, he added, 'Don't suppose, because I counsel firmness and decision at the right moment, that I am of that school of statesmen who are favourable to a turbulent and aggressive diplomacy. I have resisted it during a great part of my life. I am not unaware that the relations of England and Europe are not the same as they were in the days of Lord Chatham or Frederick the Great. The Queen of England has become the Sovereign of the most powerful of Oriental States. On the other side of the globe there are new establishments belonging to her, teeming with wealth and population, which will, in due time, exercise their influence over the distribution of power. The old establishments of this country, now the United States of America, throw their lengthening shadows over the Atlantic, which mix with European waters. These are vast and novel elements in the distribution of power.

'I acknowledge that the policy of England with respect to Europe should be a policy of reserve, but proud reserve; and in answer to those statesmen, those mistaken statesmen, who have intimated the decay of the power of England and the decline of her resources, I express here my confident conviction that there never was a moment in our history when the power of England was so great and her resources so vast and inexhaustible.

'And yet, gentlemen, it is not merely our fleets and armies, our powerful artillery, our accumulated capital, and our unlimited credit on which I so much depend, as upon that unbroken spirit of her people, which I believe was never prouder of the Imperial country to which they belong.' (Speech at Manchester, 3 April 1872.)

Conservatism and Empire   In June 1872, speaking to Conservatives at a banquet in the Crystal Palace, Disraeli made a famous declaration which was to influence the party's thinking about the British Empire for many years to come: 'If you look to the history of this country since the advent of Liberalism—forty years ago—you will find that there has been no effort so continuous, so subtle, supported by so much energy, and carried on with so much ability and acumen, as the attempts of Liberalism to effect the disintegration of the Empire or England ...

'Well, that result was nearly accomplished. When those subtle views were adopted by the country under the plausible plea of granting self-government to the Colonies, I confess that I myself thought that the tie was broken. Not that I for one object to self-government; I cannot conceive how our distant Colonies can have their affairs administered except by self-government.'

He went on: 'But self-government, in my opinion, when it was conceded, ought to have been conceded as part of a great policy of Imperial consolidation. It ought to have been accompanied by an Imperial tariff, by securities for the people of England for the enjoyment of the unappropriated lands which belonged to the Sovereign as their trustee, and by a military code which should have precisely defined the means and the responsibilities by which the Colonies should be defended, and by which, if necessary, this country should call for aid from the Colonies themselves. It ought, further, to have been accompanied by the institution of some

To Disraeli the key to India was the Suez Canal. In buying the shares from the Khedive of Egypt he ensured that Britain held on to it

representative council in the metropolis, which would have brought the Colonies into constant and continuous relations with the Home Government.

'All this, however, was omitted because those who advised that policy—and I believe their convictions were sincere—looked upon the Colonies of England, looked even upon our connection with India, as a burden upon this country; viewing everything in a financial aspect, and totally passing by those moral and political considerations which make nations great, and by the influence of which alone men are distinguished from animals.

'Well, what has been the result of this attempt during the reign of Liberalism for the disintegration of the Empire? It has entirely failed. But how has it failed? Through the sympathy of the Colonies for the Mother Country. They have decided that the Empire shall not be destroyed; and in my opinion no Minister in this country will do his duty who neglects any opportunity of reconstructing as much as possible our Colonial Empire, and of responding to those distant sympathies which may become the source of incalculable strength and happiness to this land.'

Suez Canal

Late in 1875, while Parliament was not in session, Disraeli seized an opportunity to buy a large block of shares in the Suez Canal, which had been opened in 1896. He saw this as a way of securing control over this new route to India, thereby strengthening the Empire.

In a letter to the Queen, dated 18 November 1875, Disraeli wrote: 'Mr Disraeli with his humble duty to your Majesty: The Khedive, on the eve of bankruptcy, appears desirous of parting with his shares in the Suez Canal, and communicated, confidentially, with General Stanton. There is a French company in negotiation with His Highness, but they purpose only to make an advance with complicated stipulations.

''Tis an affair of millions, about four at least. But would give the possessor an immense, not to say preponderating, influence in the management of the Canal.

'It is vital to your Majesty's authority and power at this critical moment, that the Canal should belong to England, and I was so decided and absolute with Lord Derby on this head, that he ultimately adopted my views and brought the matter before the Cabinet yesterday. The Cabinet was unanimous in their decision, that the interest of the Khedive should, if possible, be obtained, and we telegraphed accordingly ...

'The Khedive now says, that it is absolutely necessary that he should have between three and four millions sterling by the 30th of this month!

'Scarcely breathing time! But the thing must be done.'

Queen Victoria replied by telegram the next day: 'The Queen thanks Mr Disraeli for his letters. She has telegraphed her approval of the course he intends pursuing respecting the Suez Canal, but fears it will be difficult to arrange.'

On 24 November 1875 Disraeli wrote back: 'It is just settled: you have it, Madam. The French Government has been out-generaled. They tried too much, offering loans at an usurious rate, and with conditions which would have virtually given them the government of Egypt.

'The Khedive, in despair and disgust, offered your Majesty's Government to purchase his shares outright. He never would listen to such a proposition before.

'Four millions sterling!—and almost immediately. There was only one firm that could do it, Rothschilds. They behaved admirably; advanced the money at a low rate, and the entire interest of the Khedive is now yours, Madam.'

Many Liberals, including Lord Hartington who now led them in the Commons, approved the purchase, but Gladstone spoke out strongly against it.

Disraeli pleased the Queen when he suggested that she should *Empress of* assume the title of Empress of India and she encouraged him to *India* bring forward a Royal Titles Bill. When this was done, in 1876, there was much opposition to the idea. Was 'Empress' an appropriate title? Why had India been singled out for special treatment? Gladstone made a vehement speech against the Bill at its Second Reading. Victoria was sadly puzzled by the critics and especially by the behaviour of the Liberals who, having abstained from voting at the Second Reading, then decided to oppose it going to Committee.

On 17 March 1876, the Queen wrote to Disraeli: 'The Queen is greatly rejoiced at the majority last night, which she learnt on getting up this morning … She cannot but regret the extraordinary and to her incomprehensible and mistaken course of the Opposition. She concludes that in the House of Lords there will be little trouble.'

She added, in a letter written the next day: 'The Queen thinks, now that the Government have so triumphantly carried the Titles Bill in the House of Commons, it would be of great importance (as many really excellent, loyal people will not understand it, and are full of apprehension) if Mr Disraeli, at the last stage of the Bill in the House of Commons, would state strongly and clearly that it

E

was, and always had been, the Queen's wish that the title of Empress of India which had been constantly colloquially used, should apply *only* to *India* and that the title of Sovereign of the British Empire was *always* to remain what it was now, *viz.*, Queen (or in future times King) of "Great Britain and Ireland", the other being added on at the end.'

Lord Beaconsfield In August 1876 Disraeli agreed to accept a peerage. In future, as Earl of Beaconsfield, he would lead the Conservatives from the House of Lords. *Punch* had a cartoon which showed the Queen, wearing the Imperial Crown, handing a coronet to the kneeling figure of Disraeli.

This rhyme also appeared in *Punch* on 26 August 1876:

> And so the Session with a Title ends,
> That with a Title ope'd; but how unlike
> This Title unto that! *This* Title given,
> Ungrudged and uncontested, unto one
> Whom, howsoever differing men and minds
> May differ in their judgment of the man,
> All own a fighter who has fairly won
> The meed of honour which now crowns his age:
> Like some great argosy, that after years
> Of buffeting with winds and waves and wars,
> Crowned with the memories of conflicts past,
> Passes from high seas' strife to harbour's calm.

On 16 August 1876, Gladstone wrote to Sir Arthur Gordon: 'Disraeli assumes his earldom amidst loud acclaims. I had better be mute about him and his influence generally, except as to a full acknowledgement of his genius and his good points of character. His Government is supposed now to stand mainly upon its recent foreign policy: the most selfish and least worthy I have ever known. Whatever was open to any degree of exception in Palmerston, has this year received a ten-fold development in Disraeli.'

Opposite 'New Crowns for Old', or promotion from Queen to Empress with the help of the geni Disraeli

11 Conservatism in Action

THE MOST IMPORTANT PROBLEM in foreign affairs occurring during Lord Beaconsfield's Ministry was the trouble in the Balkans. This became known as the 'Eastern Question'. Twenty years before, at the end of the Crimean War, a congress of European powers had met in Paris to draw up a peace treaty. The powers then guaranteed the integrity of the Turkish Empire, so long as the Sultan carried out reforms for his Christian subjects. The Sultan, however, did little about his promise and there was continuous unrest in the Turkish provinces.

Although Beaconsfield was personally pre-occupied with foreign affairs, the Government did bring a number of useful domestic measures before Parliament. But we will look first at the Eastern question.

Twenty years after the end of the Crimean War a new crisis with Russia broke out. The subject nations of South-Eastern Europe rose up against their Turkish rulers and so gave the Russians an excuse to attack Turkey in defence of the Balkan Christians. Lord Beaconsfield, who did not wish to encourage Russia, played down reports of Turkish cruelties. Gladstone, who now threw himself wholeheartedly into parliamentary affairs again, attacked the Prime Minister and published a famous pamphlet, *The Bulgarian Horrors and the Question of the East*. As a result of his efforts, Gladstone re-established himself as the outstanding Liberal in Parliament.

Eastern question

In a speech to Members of the House of Commons on 11 August 1876, Lord Beaconsfield warned: 'We must not jump at conclusions so quickly as is now the fashion. There is nothing to justify

Opposite A conference at Constantinople to discuss the eastern question, the gravest foreign problem of Disraeli's second ministry

us in talking in such a vein of Turkey as has been, and is being at this moment, entertained. The present is a state of affairs which requires the most vigilant examination and the most careful management. But those who suppose that England ever would uphold, or at this moment particularly is upholding, Turkey from blind superstition, and from want of sympathy with the highest aspirations of humanity, are deceived.

'What our duty is at this critical moment is to maintain the Empire of England. Nor will we agree to any step, though it may obtain for a moment comparative quiet and a false prosperity, that hazards the existence of that Empire.'

Gladstone wrote many years later: 'When, in 1876, the eastern question was forced forward by the disturbances in the Turkish empire, and especially by the cruel outrages in Bulgaria, I shrank naturally but perhaps unduly from recognising the claim they made upon me individually. I hoped that the Ministers would recognise the moral obligations to the subject races of the east, which we had in honour contracted as parties to the Crimean War and to the peace of Paris in 1856. I was slow to observe the real leanings of the Prime Minister, his strong sympathy with the Turk, and his mastery in his own Cabinet ...

'At the close of the session (1876) a debate was raised upon the subject, and I had at length been compelled to perceive that the old idol was still to be worshipped at Constantinople, and that, as the only person surviving in the House of Commons who had been responsible for the Crimean War ... I could no longer remain indifferent.

'From that time forward, till the final consummation in 1879–80, I made the eastern question the main business of my life. I acted under a strong sense of individual duty without a thought of leadership; nevertheless it made me leader whether I would or no.'

In *The Bulgarian Horrors and Question of the East* Gladstone wrote: 'An old servant of the Crown and State, I entreat my countrymen, upon whom far more than perhaps any other people of Europe it depends, to require and to insist that our Government which has been working in one direction shall work in the other, and shall apply all its vigour to concur with the other states of

Turkish recruits arrive in Constantinople to be armed for the suppression of Turkey's rebellious subject states

Europe in obtaining the extinction of the Turkish executive power in Bulgaria. Let the Turks now carry away their abuses in the only possible manner, namely by carrying off themselves.'

Beaconsfield, however, dismissed the pamphlet. He mentioned Lord Derby: 'Gladstone has had the impudence to send me his pamphlet, tho' he accuses me of several crimes. The document is passionate and not strong; vindictive and ill-written—that of course.' (8 September 1876.)

Beaconsfield believed that Gladstone's anti-Turkish policy was in danger of involving Europe in the 'havoc and ruin' of a major war. In a speech at Aylesbury he said that a 'great portion of the people of this country' had been misled. He admired the noble sympathy shown by these Englishmen, but feared that 'designing politicians might take advantage of such sublime sentiments, and apply them for the furtherance of their sinister ends'.

Aylesbury speech

'I am quite convinced that Mr Gladstone on reflection never intended anything of the kind. If he had gone to the House of Commons and had proposed to the House of Commons and the

103

Mostar in Herzegovina, a scene of the rebellion against the Turks in 1875

Speaker to attend Greenwich Fair, and go to the top of Greenwich Hill and all roll down to the bottom, I declare he could not have proposed anything more absurdly incongruous.' (20 September 1876.)

As the war between Russia and Turkey dragged on, British opinion began to change. Englishmen admired the plucky resistance of the Turks, while they became increasingly alarmed by the progress made by the Russians, who looked as though they were about to take Constantinople.

Beaconsfield wrote to Queen Victoria during July 1877. 'There is one point which Lord Beaconsfield would humbly place before your Majesty. Lord Beaconsfield ventures to remark, that he has never at any time represented to your Majesty that, if the present state of neutrality were maintained, your Majesty could prevent the Russians from occupying Constantinople. That would require war with Russia, a force of 60,000 to 80,000 men at Constantinople and the British fleet.

'What he always recommended was, that the Dardanelles

should be occupied, while still professing neutrality, and held as a material guarantee for the obligations and respect of treaties. This would not have prevented the occupation of Constantinople were the Russians strong enough to effect it, but it would have given us a commanding position at the time of negotiations for peace, which would have ensured the restoration of Constantinople by the Russians and maintained untouched England's present position in the Mediterranean.'

A strong anti-Russian feeling now began to develop in the *Russophobia* country. Here is a music-hall song, popular at this time:

'We don't want to fight, but by Jingo if we do
We've got the men, we've got the ships, we've got the money too.
We've fought the Bear before, and while Britons shall be true,
The Russians shall not have Constantinople.'

And Beaconsfield stated in a telegram to the Queen on 21 July 1877: 'The Cabinet has agreed unanimously, if Russia occupies Constantinople, and does not arrange for her immediate retirement from it, to advise your Majesty to declare war against that Power. Orders have been given to strengthen the Mediterranean garrisons.'

Early in 1878 an armistice was declared between Russia and *Congress of* Turkey. This eased the tension for a time, but as soon as the terms *Berlin* of the peace agreement (Treaty of San Stefano) were made known, it rose rapidly again. The extension of Russian power alarmed many European powers. Beaconsfield demanded that the terms be put before a European Congress for review. The statesmen of Germany and Austria-Hungary agreed.

The Congress of Berlin was a great personal triumph for the British Prime Minister. Russia consented to hand back some of the territories which she had gained at San Stefano. Britain, in return for guaranteeing Turkey's remaining Eastern possessions, was given Cyprus.

Punch reported: 'Our representatives at the Congress, the EARL OF BEACONSFIELD and the MARQUIS OF SALISBURY met with an enthusiastic reception on their arrival in London, and the Order of the Garter was confirmed on both these statesmen almost immediately by Her Majesty.

105

The crowds at Charing Cross Station, London, as Disraeli triumphantly returns from the Congress of Berlin

'The existence of the Convention between England and Turkey ... was known in June, but its provisions were not published until 8 July, a few days before the close of the Congress. The principal article was to the following effect:

' "If Batoum, Ardahan, Kars, or any of them shall be retained by Russia, and if any attempt shall be made at any future time by Russia to take possession of any further territories of his Imperial Majesty the SULTAN in Asia, as fixed by the definitive Treaty of Peace, England engages to join the SULTAN in defending them by force of arms.

'In return the SULTAN promises to England to introduce necessary reforms to be agreed upon later between the two Powers, into the Government; and, for the protection of the Christian and other subjects of the Porte in these territories, and in order to enable England to make necessary provision for executing her

New model dwellings in London, part of the Conservative party's drive
towards social reform

engagements, the SULTAN further consents to assign the Island of
Cyprus, to be occupied and administered by England."

'The cession of Cyprus to this country excited much attention
and controversy, and many questions were asked in Parliament on
the subject, and also on the reported unhealthiness of the Island,
its harbour accommodation, etc. Possession was taken of Cyprus
in the name of the QUEEN in July, and before the end of the month
SIR GARNET WOLSELEY had been installed as Governor and
Commander of the Forces.'

Meantime, the Conservative Ministry carried through a number
of important social reforms. The main work was done by the
Home Secretary, Richard Cross.

Social reforms

The Artisans' Dwellings Act (1875) allowed local authorities,
for the first time, to carry out slum clearance projects. Richard
Cross told the House of Commons on 8 February 1875: 'I take it

Artisans' Dwellings Act (1875)

Samuel Plimsoll addresses the Commons during his struggle to improve conditions for merchant sailors

as a starting-point that it is not the duty of the Government to provide any class of citizens with any of the necessaries of life, and among the necessaries of life we must include that which is one of the chief necessaries—good and habitable dwellings. That it is not the duty of the State, because if it did so, it would inevitably tend to make that class depend, not on themselves, but upon what was done for them elsewhere, and it would not be possible to teach a worse lesson than this—that "If you do not take care of yourselves, the State will take care of you". Nor is it wise to encourage large bodies to provide the working classes with habitations at greatly lower rents than the market value paid elsewhere.

Public Health Act (1875) The Public Health Act (1875) brought together many health laws which had been passed in recent years.

Union reforms The Conspiracy and Protection of Property Act (1875) made peaceful picketing lawful, and gave a body of strikers the same rights as held by any one person: 'An agreement or combination [to do] any act in contemplation or furtherance of a trade dispute between employers and workmen shall not be indictable as a conspiracy if such act committed by one person would not be punishable as a crime.' (13 August 1875.)

Other Conservative social legislation included a Factory Act (1874), Employers and Workmen Act (1875), Education Act (1876) and the Rivers Pollution Act (1876).

The Government ran into trouble over its Merchant Shipping Bill (1875). This bill was the result of pressure by Samuel Plimsoll, who wanted to reduce the loss of life among seamen. His most novel idea was that a load-line be painted on the side of every ship. Influential shipowners protested, since they wanted to load as much cargo as they could.

Plimsoll line

Even Plimsoll was dissatisfied with the proposed legislation. The Bill passed its Second Reading in the Commons, but a few weeks later Disraeli decided to withdraw it; he said that the House did not have enough time to deal with it. Plimsoll raged in the House against the Prime Minister, and his dismay was soon echoed throughout the country. The Government hastily brought in a 'stop-gap' Bill, followed in 1876 by a Merchant Shipping Act.

12 The Great Duel Ends

BY 1879 the Conservatives' stock in the country was low. The Opposition continued to attack Beaconsfield's foreign policy which had led to British troops fighting in Afghanistan and against the Zulus in South Africa. But it was the depressed state of agriculture that told more heavily against the Government.

On 28 March 1879 in a speech in the House of Lords, Lord Beaconsfield said: 'No one can deny that the depression of the agricultural interest is excessive. Though I can recall several periods of suffering, none of them have ever equalled the present in its intenseness ... The remarkable feature of the present agricultural depression is this—that the agricultural interest is suffering from a succession of bad harvests, and that these bad harvests are accompanied for the first time by extremely low prices ... In old days, when we had a bad harvest, we had also the somewhat dismal compensation of higher prices. That is not the condition of the present; on the contrary the harvests are bad, and the prices are lower.'

Gladstone realised that the Liberals had a good chance of winning the next election. This could not be far off. He wrote to Lord Granville on 6 August 1879: 'Salisbury's speech indicates, and for several reasons I should believe, that they [the Conservatives] intend sailing on the quiet tack. Having proved their spirit, they will now show their moderation. In other words they want all the past proceedings to be in the main "stale fish" at the elections. Except financial shuffling they will very likely commit no new enormity before the election. In my view that means they will not supply any new matter of such severe condemnation as what they have already furnished.

111

Opposite English troops going ashore at Durban, South Africa, on their way to the Zulu War, 1879

'Therefore, my idea is, we should keep the old alive and warm. This is the meaning of my suggestion as to autumn work, rather than that I expect a dissolution. It seems to me a good policy to join on the proceedings of 1876–9 by a continuous process to the dissolution. Should this happen, which I think likely enough about March, there will have been no opportunity immediately before it of stirring the country.'

Gladstone decided to contest Midlothian, which was a Conservative seat. In November, with the election date still unknown, Gladstone embarked on a famous campaign. It was to prove a great personal triumph: 'People came from the Hebrides to hear Mr Gladstone speak. Where there were six thousand seats, the applications were forty or fifty thousand ... Mr Gladstone's counsels may have been wise or unwise, but the only flattery in the Midlothian speeches was the manly flattery contained in the fact that he took care to address all these multitudes of weavers, farmers, villagers, artisans, just as he would have addressed the House of Commons—with the same breadth and accuracy of knowledge, the same sincerity of interest, the same scruple in right reasoning, and the same appeal to the gravity and responsibility of public life.'

Midlothian campaign

The following March, as Gladstone had predicted, Beaconsfield advised the Queen to dissolve Parliament. A general election now took place.

Election of 1880

In his letter to the Queen (6 March 1880) Beaconsfield wrote: 'The Cabinet just concluded, sat two hours and a half, and every member of it was requested to give his opinion: the members of the House of Commons having the priority. There were various views, and some differences of opinion, but the ultimate result was unanimity.

'The question, after exhausting arguments, really resolved itself to this: whether your Majesty should be advised to dissolve Parliament now, or in the late autumn. The latter alternative was thought to involve too many risks; and perhaps was altogether impracticable, for the excitement of the existing House of Commons could hardly be restrained till that later period.'

Beaconsfield wrote to Lady Bradford explaining: 'I have not written before, for I have not a word to say. As for news about the

Opposite Excited crowds at West Calder, Scotland, wait to see Gladstone during his Midlothian campaign, 1879

elections, that no longer exists. All you hear now is mere speculation and gossip. The seed is sown, and we must wait for the harvest: I hope our electoral one will be better than our agricultural.' (29 March 1880.)

Gladstone was amongst the few politicians—Conservatives and Liberals alike—who anticipated the sweeping victory which his party would have.

Disraeli defeated
On 2 April 1880, Disraeli wrote of his defeat to Queen Victoria: 'Lord Beaconsfield with his humble duty to your Majesty. He has already, by a cyphered telegram this morning, had the honour to apprise your Majesty of his general view of the result of the election. He believes that the counties, by their decision, will ensure to your Majesty, in the Government of your Majesty's Dominions, the advantage of a powerful Opposition.

'It is true the farmers are suffering and are discontented, but they always have difficulty in moving and combining. On the present occasion events have been too quick for them, and, with returning prosperity, they will, in a season or two, revert to their ancient loyalty and love of order.' He concluded, 'Lord Beaconsfield attributes the cause of the present disaster to that sympathy for change which is inherent in man.'

Meanwhile, Gladstone quietly rejoiced. He wrote to the Duke of Argyll on 12 April 1880: 'All our heads are still in a whirl from the great events of the last fortnight, which have given joy, I am convinced, to the large majority of the civilized world. The downfall of Beaconsfieldism is like the vanishing of some vast magnificent castle in an Italian romance. It is too big, however, to be all taken in at once. Meantime, while I inwardly rejoice, I am against all outward signs, beyond such as are purely local, of exultation, for they are not chivalrous, and they would tend to barbarise political warfare. We may be well content to thank God in silence. But the outlook is tremendous!'

Gladstone's triumph
Who would now become Prime Minister? Lord Granville, in the Lords, was the acknowledged leader of Gladstone's old party; Lord Hartington still led the Liberals in the Commons. Neither statesman, however, could command the support which Gladstone had won during recent months by his persistent criticisms of Lord Beaconsfield and the Conservatives.

'The old head-gardener and the new': *Punch*'s view of problems facing
Gladstone on his return to power in 1880

Victoria hesitated. She did not really want Gladstone back. She
decided to speak first to Hartington. On 22 April 1880, Gladstone
wrote: 'At 7 *pm* Hartington came to see me at Wolverton's house
and reported on his journey to Windsor.

'The Queen stood with her back to the window—which *used* not
to be her custom. On the whole I gathered that her manner was
more or less embarrassed, but towards him not otherwise than
gracious and confiding. She told him that she desired him to form
an administration, and pressed upon him strongly his duty to
assist her as a responsible leader of the party now in a large
majority. I could not find that she expressed clearly her reason for
appealing to him as a responsible leader of the party, and yet

115

going past *the* leader of the party, namely Granville, whom no one except himself has a title to displace ...

'Hartington, in reply to her Majesty, ... did not think a government could be satisfactorily formed without me; but he had reason to believe that I would not take any office or post in the government except of first minister. Under those circumstances he advised her Majesty to place the matter in my hands.'

The next day Gladstone wrote: 'Soon after half-past three today, Lord Granville and Lord Hartington arrived from Windsor at my house, and signified to me the Queen's command that I should repair to Windsor, where she would see me at half-past six.' Power came once again to Gladstone.

Beaconsfield dies

On 23 March 1881, the British public heard that Lord Beaconsfield had been taken ill. What at first was reported as a 'slight cold' became within a few days a severe 'attack of bronchial asthma' and there was a growing concern about his health. On 30 March 1881, *The Standard* gravely reported: 'The news of Lord Beaconsfield's illness has been received by every section of the public with deep concern and regret ...'

It went on to say: 'Less than a year has passed since Lord Beaconsfield was Prime Minister. The position which he now fills, in point of honour and influence, is subordinate only to that of the Premier himself. The First Lord of the Treasury and the Leader of Her Majesty's Opposition are the two great terms in the equation of political power in England. The one can as little be an irresponsible statesman as the other. No one has ever shown a deeper conviction of this truth than Lord Beaconsfield, nor is there any other respect than this in which his mere political superiority to Mr Gladstone has more conspicuously made itself felt.'

Lord Beaconsfield's death was announced in a Bulletin of 19 April 1881: 'The debility, which was evidently increasing yesterday, progressed during the night, and Lord Beaconsfield died at half-past four this morning, calmly, as if in sleep.'

Gladstone's tribute

In his letter of 19 April 1881, to Lord Rawton, Gladstone wrote: 'It was with sad surprise after more favourable accounts of successive days down to yesterday morning that I learned this day at an early hour the decease of Lord Beaconsfield, which will be

116

Opposite Disraeli (Lord Beaconsfield) photographed towards the end of his life

regarded with so much mournful interest throughout the country and beyond its limits.

'In conformity with the message I have already sent, I desire at once to inform you and his executors, that if it should be agreeable to their wishes, I shall be prepared to give the necessary directions for a public funeral.'

The offer was declined, a public funeral being against Lord Beaconsfield's wishes. He had written in his will: 'I desire and direct that I may be buried in the same vault, in the churchyard of Hughenden, in which the remains of my late dear wife, Mary Anne Disraeli, created in her own right Viscountess Beaconsfield, were placed, and that my funeral may be conducted with the same simplicity as hers was.'

When Parliament reassembled after the Easter recess, both Houses voted for a monument to the memory of Lord Beaconsfield. Gladstone proposed the motion in the Commons 'with taste and dignity': 'The career of Lord Beaconsfield is, in many respects, the most remarkable one in Parliamentary history ... I feel myself in the position, not necessarily of a friend and admirer, who looks with sympathy at the character and action of Lord Beaconsfield, but I look at the magnitude of the part which he played on behalf of his country ...' *Praise from his opponent*

Gladstone continued: 'There is much error and misapprehension abroad as to the personal sentiments that prevail between men who are divided in politics. Their words must necessarily from time to time be sharp; their judgments may occasionally, may warrantably, may necessarily be severe; but the general idea of persons less informed than those within the Parliamentary circle is that they are actuated towards one another by sentiments of intense antipathy or hatred. *Gladstone's relations with Disraeli*

'I wish to take this occasion, with the permission of the House— if for a moment I may degenerate into egoism upon a subject much too high for it—I wish to record in this place and at this hour my firm conviction that in all the judgments ever delivered by the late Lord Beaconsfield on myself, he was never actuated by sentiments of personal antipathy.' (9 May 1881.)

In a private memorandum (March 1894) Gladstone reflected: 'Politics are like a labyrinth, from the inner intricacies of which it *'The grand old man'*

Opposite 'The Old Man', as Gladstone was affectionately known in his old age

is even more difficult to find the way of escape, than it was to find the way into them.'

William Ewart Gladstone did not find his own political 'escape' until 1894, after more than sixty years as a member of the House of Commons. During that period he had served as Prime Minister four times. It is not surprising that people called him the 'grand old man' of British politics.

Gladstone's dies, 1898

The later events in his long life lie outside the scope of this book. Let us close these pages with the words of two parliamentary colleagues spoken in tribute on the day after his death. In a speech in the House of Lords, Lord Salisbury recalled: 'He had qualities that distinguished him from all other men; and you may say that it was his transcendent intellect, his astonishing power of attaching men to him, and the great influence he was able to exert upon the thought and convictions of his contemporaries.

What he sought were the attainments of great ideals, and, whether they were based on sound convictions or not, they could have issued from nothing but the greatest and the purest moral aspirations; and he is honoured by his countrymen, because through so many years, across so many vicissitudes and conflicts, they had recognised this one characteristic of his action, which has never ceased to be felt ... he will be long remembered not so much for the causes in which he was engaged or the political projects which he favoured, but as a great example, to which history hardly furnishes a parallel, of a great Christian man.'

A man of dignity And speaking in the House of Commons, Arthur Balfour declared: 'One service he did, in my opinion incalculable, which is altogether apart from the judgment that we may be disposed to pass upon particular opinions, or particular lines of policy which Mr Gladstone may from time to time have advocated. Sir, he added a dignity, as he added a weight, to the deliberations of this House by his genius, which I think it is impossible adequately to replace.'

Prime Ministers

1828–30	Duke of Wellington (Tory)
1830–34	Earl Grey (Whig)
1834	Lord Melbourne (Whig)
1834–5	Sir Robert Peel (Tory)
1835–41	Lord Melbourne (Whig)
1841–6	Sir Robert Peel (Tory)
1846–52	Lord John Russell (Whig)
1852	Lord Derby (Conservative)
1852–5	Lord Aberdeen (Whig—Peelite Coalition)
1855–8	Lord Palmerston (Whig)
1858–9	Lord Derby (Conservative)
1859–65	Lord Palmerston (Whig—Peelite Coalition)
1865–6	Lord John Russell (Liberal)
1866–8	Lord Derby (Conservative)
1868	Benjamin Disraeli (Conservative)
1868–74	William Gladstone (Liberal)
1874–80	Benjamin Disraeli (Conservative)
1880–5	William Gladstone (Liberal)
1885–6	Lord Salisbury (Conservative)
1886	William Gladstone (Liberal)
1886–92	Lord Salisbury (Conservative)
1892–4	William Gladstone (Liberal)
1894–5	Lord Rosebery (Liberal)
1895–1902	Lord Salisbury (Conservative)

Table of Events

Second Government
1859 Gladstone is again Chancellor of Exchequer—Palmerston's Second Government
1860 Cobden's Treaty
1861 American Civil War begins
1862 Gladstone's Newcastle speech in which he appears to recognise the South
1865 Death of Palmerston
1867 Reform Act
1868 Disraeli is Prime Minister
Gladstone is Prime Minister
1869 Irish Church Act
Suez Canal opened
1870 Education Act
Irish Land Act
Franco-Prussian War
1871 Army reforms
Trade Union Act
1872 Ballot Act
Licensing Act
Disraeli's speech at Crystal Palace
1874 Disraeli's Second Ministry
1875 Purchase of Suez Canal shares
Artisans' Dwellings Act
Public Health Act
Conspiracy and Protection of Property Act
1876 Merchant Shipping Act
Eastern crisis
Gladstone condemns the Bulgarian atrocities
Victoria becomes Empress of India
Disraeli created Lord Beaconsfield
1877 Russo-Turkish War
1878 Congress of Berlin—a 'triumph' for Disraeli
1879 Gladstone's Midlothian campaign
1880 Gladstone's Second Ministry
1881 Death of Lord Beaconsfield—buried at Hughenden
1894 Gladstone retires from Parliament
1898 Death of Gladstone—buried in Westminster Abbey

Picture Credits

The Publishers wish to thank the following for permission to reproduce the illustrations on the pages mentioned: the Trustees of the National Portrait Gallery, jacket, 34, 91; the Weaver-Smith Collection, 13, 15, 17, 25, 28, 31, 33, 36, 38, 40, 42, 45 (*above right and bottom*), 54, 57, 60, 64, 68, 72, 76-77, 82, 83, 99, 100, 103, 108; the Mansell Collection, *frontispiece*, 52, 58, 81, 86, 95, 115, 117. Other illustrations appearing in this book are the property of the Wayland Picture Library.

Further Reading

ABOUT GLADSTONE AND DISRAELI

The most comprehensive biographies are:
Monypenny, W. F., Buckle, G. E., *The Life of Benjamin Disraeli*, 6 Vols (John Murray)
Morley, J., *The Life of William Ewart Gladstone*, 3 Vols (Macmillan)

For something much shorter, and containing illustrations, see:
Blake, R. N. W., *Disraeli* (OUP)
Collieu, E. G., *Gladstone* (OUP)

ABOUT PARLIAMENT

Derry, J., *Parliamentary Reform* (Macmillan)
—, *Political Parties* (Macmillan)
  (These two books are specially written for young people.)
Evans, R. H., *Government* (Vista). Contains more than two hundred illustrations
Oxford Junior Encyclopaedia, Vol 10 (OUP). This volume, *Law and Society*, deals with many aspects of parliamentary government.

BACKGROUND HISTORIES

Cammiade, A., *Victoria's Reign* (Methuen)
Derry, T. K., and Jarman, T. L., *The Making of Modern Britain* (John Murray)
Neuth, A. M., *Britain and the World 1789–1901* (Penguin Educational)
Pike, E., Royston, *Human Documents of the Victorian Golden Age* (Allen & Unwin)

Reader, W. J., *Life in Victorian England* (Batsford)

Rooke, P., *Agriculture and Industry* (Rupert Hart-Davis)

Trevelyan, G. M., *Illustrated English Social History*, Vol. IV (Longmans)

NOVELS

The following list is but a small sample of the many novels which were written during this period, and which provide authentic background reading:

Dickens, C., *Pickwick Papers*. This describes the election scene at Eatanswill.

—, *Our Mutual Friend*. Introduces Hamilton Veneering, MP.

Disraeli, B., *Sybil* and *Coningsby*. Both reflect the spirit of the 'Young Englanders'.

Eliot, G., *Silas Marner*

Gaskell, E., *Mary Barton*

Kingsley, C., *Alton Locke*

Trollope, A., *Barchester Towers*

MISCELLANEOUS

In addition, bound copies of contemporary journals are a useful source of fascinating material, notably *Punch*, and the *Illustrated London News*.

Index